GOOD HOUSEKEEPING

FRENCH COOKERY

GOOD HOUSEKEEPING

FRENCH COOKERY

HELGE RUBINSTEIN

EBURY PRESS

Published by Ebury Press
National Magazine House
72 Broadwick Street
London W1V 2BP

First impression 1981

ISBN 0 85223 197 0

Design by Design 23
Artist Susanne Lihou
Photography Paul Kemp

Filmset in Great Britain by
Servis Filmsetting Ltd
Manchester, England
Printed and bound in Italy by
New Interlitho s.p.a. Milan

Contents

Introduction

A journey through France is a feast for all the senses. It is a country of great variety and contrast, rich in history. In France every region has its own specialities – in food as much as in landscape and architecture.

A land the size of France, with three distinct coastlines, two mountain ranges – the Alps and the Pyrenees – at opposite corners, as well as the Massif Central in the middle, has a wide range of climatic conditions. Wherever you go, therefore, the local produce has its own special characteristics, and so has the cuisine, for the French cook, be it housewife or chef, has a fine respect for raw materials, and the cooking will be designed to make the best of what is available locally.

In *Good Housekeeping French Cookery*, we have divided our exploration into two parts. The introduction takes us on a tour through the bounty of France, from the flat, northeast corner of Flanders, through the rocky coastline of Western Brittany, to the salt-marshes of the Carmargue in the South. These pages constitute a roving appreciation of the meat and game, vegetables, fruit and cheeses of the world's most favoured cuisine. They are followed by pages of recipes which enable armchair travellers to bring the richness of France into their kitchens. Each recipe – whether first course, main course, side dish or dessert – has the region of its origin noted below the name. And given some careful saving, preliminary planning and a good deal of anticipation, there is nothing to stop the peripatetic reader from taking this wide but specialised knowledge of French regional cooking as the basis for gastronomic forays into the mother country itself.

We begin in Brittany, with its megalithic stones and roadside calvaries, and above all, its varied coastline. At times rocky and perilous, at others flat and marshy, it provides an abundance of seafood and shellfish. On to neighbouring Normandy, country of lush pastures and rich dairy products, as well as home of William the Conqueror and the Bayeax tapestry. The soaring Gothic cathedrals are the pride of the north-eastern part of France, which bears the rather heavier Flemish and German influences in its cooking, with solid, warming pork and onion-based dishes, graced by the flinty wines of Alsace. Between the two lies the Île de France, with Paris, capital city of *haute cuisine* and home of great restaurants since the time of the Revolution, at its centre.

As we move further south, we come to the country of the Loire and its tributaries, with lovely chateaux reflected in the rivers. Here freshwater fish and light Loire wines predominate, while a little further down in Burgundy, in the very heart of France, we can enjoy the fine Charollais beef, the plump yellow chickens of Bresse and the great Burgundy wines. Approaching the centre of France we come to the area of the Dordogne and the great gorges of the Tarn, to the country where Romanesque churches and romantic landscapes delight the eye, and the rich pates and truffles of the Perigord are feasts for the palate.

Here we begin to meet the two chief flavours of the South, garlic and olive oil, and the further south we go, the more these two flavours dominate, coupled with the profusion of fruit and vegetables from Provence, country of Van Gogh landscapes, rich in remains from its Roman past. When we finally reach the southern coast, there is the many-splendoured seafood of the Mediterranean. Going westwards towards the Atlantic coast and along the Pyrenees, we find the Basque and Spanish influence in the cuisine, while the towns and fortresses resonate with echoes from the Middle Ages, and Roland's Roncevalles is still the pass into Spain.

No wonder that with so much local history, France is still a country of well-defined provinces. I have used their old historic names rather than the modern *département* equivalents, for these are the borders that still count from the gastronomic point of view. Even with modern methods of refrigeration and fast transport, and the growth of convenience, especially frozen, foods, which the French housewife is far too canny to despise, French cooking has retained its regional character. In spite of the fact that one of the earliest known cookery books was written by a Frenchman, the great Taillevent, master-cook to Charles VI, cookery books are used much less here than in other countries, and traditions are still handed down from mother to daughter – and from father to son.

For all its strong roots, French cooking is still breaking new ground. But although the 'nouvelle cuisine' has no place in this book, which is about the traditional cooking of provincial France, it too follows the fundamental tenet of good cooking, which is a basic respect – or love – for the raw materials. 'Faites simples' is the laconic ground-rule given by Escoffier, author of the classic '*Guide Culinaire*', and he stands well rooted in the tradition of his forebears. We have only to look at the *Trés Riches Heures du Duc de Berry* to see how lovingly the 15th-century artists portrayed the pleasures of the table. Happily, the French have no puritan tradition, and their love of food remains unrepentant.

The traveller through France – both footloose tourist and our reader – has the opportunity to share these pleasures. *Bon voyage et bon appetit.*

Brittany, Maine and Touraine

The 3,500 km-long crennelated coastline of Brittany dominates the life of the region, and the rich variety of seafood is its chief gastronomic glory. This is not an area for elaborate dishes or extravagant sauces; indeed, until the last century, Brittany was quite poor, so there is no tradition of a sophisticated cuisine.

But nothing can rival the abundance of shellfish caught all around its coast: the lobsters from the rocky promontories of the most westerly tip of France, the crabs, spider crabs, scallops, clams, langoustines and shrimps, and above all the oysters, the Belon oyster the most famous amongst them, reared in the oyster beds of the gulf of Morbihan. Brittany was one of the first areas to go in for oyster cultivation, and is still one of the few places where even the most dedicated oyster lover may be heard to say 'Oh, no, not oysters again!' Even more plentiful and less expensive than oysters are the little shiny blue-black mussels that cluster on thick posts or *buchots* set into the shallow marshy sea bed along the south-west coast, and which are harvested in special flat-bottomed boats at low tide, a method that is said to have been discovered here (by accident, like all the best inventions) by a ship-wrecked Irishman in the thirteenth century. It has changed little since. Shellfish, along with mackerel, monkfish, sole, cod and above all sardines, make the fish markets and stalls one of the most exciting places to visit in the coastal Breton towns.

Then there are the famous *pré-salé* lambs, the lambs reared in the tide-washed salty meadows around Mont St Michel, tender and tasty, and the grey sea-salt itself that is panned in that area, and which, dirty and unpromising though it may look, gives the cooking of the region some of its special flavour.

Inland Brittany also has its market gardens, and Roscoff is famous for its firm, long-lasting onions, and still sends out a fleet of bicycling onion sellers every year; Nantes prides itself on its carrots; the artichokes of St Brieuc are fat and full to bursting, and the strawberries of Plougastel are highly prized for their flavour. There are special greengages which grow in this northern part of France which owe their name to Claude of Brittany, Queen to Francois I.

Brittany's national dish is the 'crèpe', the huge buckwheat pancake which can be bought from stalls at street corners, or eaten at crèperies, specialized small restaurants where you can make a whole meal of crepes, starting with savoury fillings, and ending with a final 'crèpe au chocolat' – accompanied by the local cider.

As you move further east into Maine and Touraine, a land of kings and poets, the landscape becomes gentler and the cooking more refined. The river Loire is full of salmon, pike (most honoured in the restaurant dish, *quenelles de brochet*) shad and trout, to be served with the delicate *beurre blanc*.

This is a land of orchards and pig farms, with such farmhouse conserves as *rillettes de porc* in every charcuterie window, and fresh cheeses, such as the *cremets* of Angers, a cream cheese to be eaten with sugar and cream, and goat's cheeses, such as the famous St Maure, to be found in the markets.

A gentle cuisine, to be accompanied by the delicate, fresh Loire wines.

Normandy

Sunbaked and contented, that is how Normandy strikes the summer traveller, with its prosperous farmsteads and fertile orchards – and no hint of the fighting that has time and again swept across these fields from the Vikings onwards, right up to 1944.

Nature has been generous to Normandy. Its coastline is long and produces an enviable variety of seafood: not only the sole for which Normandy is famous, but also lobsters and langoustines, shrimps and scallops, oysters and mussels, turbot, mackerel and herring. The coast is washed by the Gulf Stream, so that the climate is temperate.

The lush pastures are grazed by sleek and placid cows, whose products are the pride of Normandy. A visit to a dairy shop is a joy. Here, in spotlessly clean, probably tiled surroundings, you will see great mounds of the freshest butter – the best is said to come from Issigny, on the north coast – deep yellow if it is slightly salted, paler if unsalted, from which you may cut a block as large or small as you wish. Stoneware jars, blue-patterned outside, grey inside, hold quantities of *crème fraîche*, the thick, slightly acidulated cream that is such a prominent feature of Norman cooking, to be ladled out and sold by weight. Here too you can buy fresh cream cheeses, such as *fromage blanc, petits suisses* and others. And, as you drive through the smaller towns and villages of Normandy, you realize that every other place sounds like a cheese – Camembert, Livarot, Pont-L'Evêque, La Bouille, Neufchâtel.

Everywhere there are apple orchards. Best of all are said to be the apples from the Vallée d'Auge, from which the many meat dishes which use apples get their name. Cider, sweet or dry, sparkling or still, is one of the chief products of the area, and every farm in the region seems to advertize its own home-made variety. In restaurants it is served throughout the meal, up to and including the dessert, which in any case is often the famous *tarte normande*.

Calvados is the eau-de-vie made from apples, and it too is often distilled and sold by individual proprietors. It is matured in casks for up to ten years, and is drunk after meals or as a *trou normand*, a digestif drunk in the middle of the meal to make room for the next course.

Benedictine, the liqueur distilled from a variety of herbs, is also a native of Normandy, and is still made near Fécamp where it was first brewed by a sixteenth century monk.

Rouen is the gastronomic capital of Normandy, and when you have marvelled at its beautiful cathedral, it is time to feast your eyes on the foodshops, notably the pâtisseries which glint and sparkle like jewellers, and the charcuteries, as amusing and as colourful as toyshops. Rouen is especially famous for its ducks, which have an almost gamey flavour. From them pâtés and galantines are made, all temptingly displayed in the charcuterie windows, together with many different kinds of sausages, especially black puddings, or *boudins*, and the famous *tripe à la mode de Caen*.

When you have spent a little time in Normandy you will no longer be surprised at Mme Bovary's wedding feast, held at Pont-Audemer, where they sat down 'forty-three to a table and remained there sixteen hours'.

Alsace, Lorraine and Franche-Comté

We are so used to thinking of Alsace and Lorraine in one breath, that we forget that they are really quite separate regions, with very different histories.

Lorraine was an independent dukedom until midway through the eighteenth century when Louis XV acquired it and made his father-in-law, Stanislas Leszczynski, the deposed king of Poland, governor and Duke of Lorraine. Not only does Nancy owe Stanislas the grace and elegance of its central square, which is named after him, but Stanislas also seems to have been responsible for many happy inventions in food. It was he who first soaked plain cakes in sweet wine or rum, and so invented the rum baba; his cook, Madeleine, is said to have been the first to make the little fluted cakes that bear her name, and it was one of his pâtissiers who thought of filling puff pastry cases with a mixture of chicken and mushrooms in cream sauce. They were sent to Marie, Stanislas' daughter, and have been known as *bouchées à la reine* ever since.

Cakes, pastry, preserves and confectionery still play a large part in the cooking of the area. There are the quiches, perhaps the best-known of the specialities of Lorraine, and also macaroons, gingerbreads and airy little doughnuts wickedly known as *pets de nonne*. Bar-le-Duc, the old seat of the dukes of Lorraine, specializes in beautiful, jewel-like fruit preserves; Metz has its *fraises de*

Metz, crystallized strawberries, and Nancy its *bergamots de Nancy*, the bergamot-flavoured little boiled sweets.

Alsace, which shares the Rhine as a border with Germany, has had many years of German domination, and the influence of Germany is very marked in the food, especially in the prominence of pork. *Choucroûte garni* is probably the best known Alsatian speciality, and a formidable dish it is, with its mountain of sauerkraut topped with smoked pork, smoked ham and the numerous different pork sausages of the region. Goose is the other great speciality, and the *pâté de foie gras* of Strasbourg is almost as famous as its cathedral.

Alsace is of course primarily a wine-growing area, and a trip through the wine villages, especially at the time of the grape harvest, is like a visit to a highly modernized Ruritania, with immaculately kept (sometimes rebuilt) mediaeval villages. The cooking here, as so often in wine-growing areas, is of the very finest, and the area around Illhaeusern is as thickly studded with Michelin stars as any in France. To end an Alsatian meal there will be an eau-de-vie, distilled from one of the many soft or stoned fruit that grow so richly here. Kirsch is the best known, but *framboise* and *myrtilles* also have a miraculous bouquet.

The Franche-Comté, further south, is a beautiful area of peaks, forests and streams familiar from the paintings of Courbet, whose homeland it was. There are fresh trout from mountain streams; crayfish, which are the basis of the coral pink *sauce Nantua*; good mountain food such as smoked sausages with picturesque names like *Jèsus* and *gendarmes*, and good hard cheeses, especially the Comté cheese which is excellent for cooking and eating alike. Perhaps the greatest pleasure of all are the many different mushrooms that can be found in the woods.

Ile de France, Paris and Orléanais

The Ile de France, with Paris at its centre, is and has been for centuries the very heart of France. It is not an area that has developed very specific characteristics of its own, but Paris is traditionally the centre of all excellence, the birth place of haute cuisine as well as of haute couture.

Since the time of the Revolution, when grand households were dissolved and some of the chefs from the nobility started the first restaurants, Paris has been the home of some of the world's most renowned *tables*, devoted to cooking as one of the fine arts. For this, it is singularly well placed, for all the best ingredients from all over the country have always been brought to the capital and have

Glossary

Follow either the metric or imperial measures for the recipes in this book as they are not interchangeable.

All spoon measurements are level, unless otherwise stated. Size 4 eggs should be used, except where otherwise stated.

Bake blind To bake flan cases, tarts and tartlet pastry cases without a filling. The pastry may be lined with greaseproof paper and dried beans, foil, or small tartlet cases may just be pricked with a fork.

Baste To moisten meat, poultry or game during roasting by spooning over it the juices and melted fat from the tin. This prevents the food from drying out, adds extra flavour and improves the appearance.

Beurre manié A liaison of butter and flour kneaded together to a paste. Used for thickening soups or stews after cooking is complete. Whisk a little of the paste into the hot liquid and bring back to the boil, adding a little more until the required thickness is reached.

Blanch To treat food with boiling water in order to whiten it; to preserve its natural colour; to loosen its skin; to remove any strong or bitter taste; to kill unwanted enzymes before freezing or preserving.

Bouquet garni A small bunch of herbs tied together in muslin and used to give flavour to stews and casseroles. A simple bouquet garni consists of a sprig each of parsley and thyme, a bay leaf, 2 cloves and a few peppercorns.

Canapés Appetisers, consisting as a rule of slices of bread cut into various sizes – usually quite small – used plain or fried, topped with savoury titbits.

Core To remove the hard, indigestible centre of certain foods, particularly fruits such as apples, pears and pineapples. The term is also used to describe removing the centre of kidneys.

Croûte 1 A large round or finger of toasted bread, about 0.5 cm ($\frac{1}{4}$ inch) thick, on which game and some entrées and savouries are served.

Croûte 2 A pastry crust.

Croûtons Small pieces of bread which are fried or toasted and served as an accompaniment to soup or as a garnish.

Crème fraîche This is cream, found widely in France which has matured and fermented to the point where it has thickened slightly and has a faintly acid taste. To make a similar substitute see page 118.

Crush To break down food into smaller particles either, as in the case of spices in a pestle and mortar, or garlic through a garlic press, to release the flavour in cooking or to make a crumb-like texture, as with biscuits, for mixing with other ingredients.

En croûte Encrusted, wrapped or enclosed in pastry before cooking.

Flake To separate cooked fish into individual flakes.

Flambé Used to describe a dish flavoured with flamed alcohol. Alcohol (usually brandy or sherry) is ignited and allowed to burn either on the finished dish or in the pan during cooking.

Glaze To give a glossy surface to sweet or savoury dishes before or after cooking. Various substances are used for different foods. The glaze improves both appearance and flavour.

flowed through its markets and shops. Moreover, the surrounding countryside of the Ile de France with its mild and even climate, is like a gigantic market garden, and almost every small district in the area has its own speciality to offer, be it a raw material or a special dish.

Some of the best potatoes and beans are grown in the area around Soissons; Crécy is so famous for its carrots that any dish with its name is enough to signify that carrots are among the ingredients. The area around Orleans, in the Loire valley, also produces some of the best green and root vegetables, and has become one of the centres of the canning industry of France. The forests around Paris and Fontainebleau have always provided plentiful game and a great variety of mushrooms, while *champignons de Paris*, the little white button mushrooms, have been cultivated in caves and disused quarries around Paris for centuries. Paris itself was once surrounded by orchards, and some of its suburbs are still full of fruit trees, especially Montmorency, well known for its fat, tart cherries.

To the south of Paris are the wheatfields of the Beauce area. You can see the great cathedral of Chartres floating in the distance above the plain as you drive towards the city. This ready supply of wheat has helped to make Paris the home of some of the best bread in the world. The Parisian *baguette*, and all its many fatter and thinner cousins, eaten within a few hours of baking with fresh Normandy butter, is quite simply one of the most delectable pleasures in life. And then there is the whole complex art of the pastry cook, nowhere more highly developed than in Paris, where every pâtissier is a craftsman, making not only his own croissants and brioches, but also éclairs, mille-feuilles, gâteaux and petits-fours.

The area has many other specialities. There is the special granular mustard in its white earthenware pot called Meaux, that derives its name from the city just north-west of Paris. There are the wild strawberries of Rambouillet; the famous cheeses from Coulommiers and from Brie – the latter dubbed 'the king of cheeses' by Talleyrand; the honey from the Gatinais area; and some of the world's best vinegar from Orléans, for it is here that vinegar was first made from wine that would not travel. From Fontainebleau come the fine Chasselas grapes, reputedly among the first to be cultivated for the table. And the town of Chantilly has given its name to the delicate light whipped cream of French pâtisseries.

No wonder that, with such surroundings, Paris has long been the gastronomic capital of Europe, Mecca for all worshippers of the table.

Joint To divide poultry, game birds or small animals such as hares and rabbits into suitable portions for cooking.

Knead To work a dough firmly, using the knuckles for bread-making, the finger-tips in pastry-making. In both cases the outside of the dough is drawn into the centre.

Knock back To knead dough for a second time on a lightly floured surface for 2–3 minutes after rising. This knocks out any large bubbles and ensures an even texture.

Langues de chats Literally cats' tongues; small, thin, flat, crisp biscuits.

Lard To insert small strips of fat bacon into the flesh of game birds, poultry and meat before cooking to prevent it drying out when roasting. A special larding needle is used. Today, because of the texture of British meat, it is usually used more for decorative effect.

Line To give a protective or decorative covering to the base and sides of a cooking container – eg. with greaseproof or non-stick paper when baking cakes; with pastry when making flans; or with bacon for pâtés.

Marinate To steep raw meat, game or fish in a blend of oil, wine or vinegar and seasonings for periods of an hour up to several days to make it more tender and flavoursome, and to give moisture to dry meats.

Mouli-légumes An inexpensive food mill found in most French kitchens, used for puréeing foods.

Pâte Pastry, especially pâte sucrée, a sweet flan pastry.

Poach To cook gently in a liquid at simmering point so that the surface is just trembling. It can be done in an open pan, in the oven or using an egg poacher with a lid. The term is used most commonly for eggs and fish.

Purée To sieve, blend or pound raw or cooked foods so that they are of a creamy, lump-free texture. If using a sieve, a wire one may be used for meat and vegetables but a nylon one is best for fruit and tomatoes.

Press To shape meat by pressing it under a weight. The cold pressed meat – often spiced meat or tongue, boned stuffed chicken or meat roll – is turned out and sometimes glazed. Some fruit desserts are also pressed.

Reduce To fast boil a liquid (especially when making a soup, sauce or syrup) in an uncovered pan, in order to evaportate surplus liquid and give a more concentrated result.

Rise To allow a yeast dough to double in size before baking. When it has risen, the dough is sometimes knocked down, shaped and then allowed to rise for a second time – also known as proving.

Scald To pour boiling water over fruit (eg. tomatoes, peaches) to make it easy to remove skins, and over pork to loosen hairs from its skin or to treat trotters. Remove food before it cooks. Also to treat milk or to cleanse jelly bags.

Skim To take off the surface of stock, garavy, stews, etc. or scum from other foods (eg. jams) while they are cooking. A piece of kitchen paper or a metal spoon may be used.

Terrine China or earthenware dish used for pâtés and potted meats, also general term for food cooked in a terrine.

Truffle A rare fungus of the same family as the mushroom. Either black or white (rarely red). Truffles are used mostly for garnishing.

Truss To tie or skewer a bird into a compact shape before cooking.

Charentes, Poitou and Limousin

The flat, silted coastline of the Charentes Maritime is a continuation of the southern coast of Brittany, and it shares much the same rich haul of Atlantic seafood as its northern neighbour – from tuna, swordfish and even sturgeon, down to sardines and tiny elvers. The speciality of La Rochelle, the big Atlantic seaport, is the *chaudrée*, from the archaic French word for cauldron – a great stew or soup made from all the fish, large and small, that come into the port. Oysters and mussels are farmed here too, and the creamy *mouclade* is as popular here as in southern Brittany, while the Ile d'Oleron, just off the coast, has the biggest shrimp fishing industry in France.

The marshy pastures just inland feed cattle and sheep, and produce *pré-salé* lamb as tender and as well flavoured as the lambs of Brittany. Further inland, large snails, called *cagouilles* grow fat in the vineyards, and '*cagouillard*' is a favourite insult to throw at the local inhabitants, accusing them of snail-like sluggishness.

The most famous product of the area is cognac, the world-renowned pure brandy made from the wine of a strictly defined area, and matured in casks of oak from neighbouring Limousin. Visitors should certainly go to see the vaults of at least one of the great brandy houses in the town of Cognac itself, belonging to Martell, Hennessy, Otard and such great names as these.

Market gardening is a flourishing local industry, producing, in particular, the famous, fragrant Charentais melons, and this is the beginning of the garlic growing and eating south.

In Poitou, in the northern part of this region, and in the Limousin, we enter a fertile area of rich farmland and market gardens, where beans, courgettes, artichokes, cauliflowers and, above all, cabbages are grown. This is an area of rich and comfortable food, with hams from the Vendée, conserves of duck and goose, game and mushrooms from the forests (the famous dish *lièvre à la royale*, which takes all day to prepare, comes from Limoges) and goat cheeses, especially the creamy Chabichou and the Pyramide from Poitou.

Above all, the area is rich in chestnuts and walnuts. Chestnut trees line the roads, to be gathered by the fistful by passers-by. They are used in every kind of dish, both sweet and savoury. There is the *purée limousine*, a purée of cabbage or sprouts and chestnuts; they are served braised as a vegetable to be eaten on its own; they are made into a flour for bread and cakes, and they are also candied to make *marrons glacés*, to export around the world. The local walnut oil, once used by painters to mix their delicate colours, is much prized. It must be used very fresh, and has a unique flavour, every bit as rich, and with a special pungency of its own, as the olive oil from further south.

Artois, Flanders, Picardy and Champagne

Artois, Flanders and Picardy are low-lying areas like their neighbour, Belgium, and the temperament of the country, as of its people, is sturdy and steady, in spite of the many scenes of fighting that have taken place over the centuries on its land and beaches.

Herring and mackerel are caught off the coast, especially around Dunkirk and Calais, and they are eaten, smoked and salted as well as fresh, in *matelotes*, or fish stews. Further along the coast, at Wimereux near Boulogne, once an elegant seaside resort, the local people pride themselves on cultivating some of the best mussels – small, dark blue, and with an excellent flavour. In the bay of Le Crotoy you can eat wonderful hors d'oeuvres of small shellfish, or jellied eels or a fish soup known in these parts as a *chaudière*.

Wild boar is still hunted in the densely wooded area of the Ardennes, and pork features prominently in the region's robust country cooking. Ardennes ham, smoked to a deep red colour, is a speciality, and pork sausages, *boudins* or blood sausages, including a special *boudin blanc*, and *andouillettes*, or tripe sausages, are eaten alone or in such hearty dishes as the *hochepot*, hefty northern cousin to the *pot au feu*. Such meals are usually accompanied by beer, for this is one of the few areas of France where no wine is grown locally.

There is other game too, and *pâté de bécasse* (woodcock pâté) and duck pie, or *canard en croûte*, are specialities of Amiens.

Vegetables are mostly root vegetables or cabbage, often cooked with the meat or made into a pie, such as the Flemish speciality, the creamy *flamiche de poireaux*.

Desserts in this area are substantial too, and tend to be tarts, fritters or puddings. But the town of Cambrai, whose fortune is based on the wool and cloth trade, has a charming speciality of delicate little mint-flavoured pillow-shaped sweets, known as *bêtises de Cambrai*, for they are said to have been a *bêtise* or mistake made by an apprentice.

The countryside of Champagne, as its name (derived from the word for field) implies, is flat, or gently hilly with wide vistas of plains, and the rivers and streams that run across it provide carp, pike and trout. The town of Rheims, with its great and historic cathedral in which the kings of France were crowned, has its speciality, a ham in pastry case, as well as a special pear called *rousselet*, which is traditionally offered to visiting monarchs or heads of state, but is too juicy to travel. The real glory of the area lies in its world famous wine, which, to be truly champagne, must be made from grapes grown in a strictly defined area. The process of making champagne was developed by a seventeenth century Benedictine monk, Dom Perignon, who was born in St. Ménéhould, now more associated with its speciality, grilled pig's trotters. The process of making champagne, which has been refined and perfected since Dom Perignon discovered a way of preserving the sparkling quality of the wine, is a long and fascinating one, and traveller in this area should visit at least one of the famous champagne houses and its *caves*.

Burgundy, Nivernais, Berry and Bourbonnais

For lovers of good food and good wine, Burgundy is a paradise on earth. Few other regions in France are so richly endowed with the products of nature, and in none has human skill embellished them so deliciously as here.

The great white Charollais cattle originate from this area and are still most at home in the lush pastureland of the Charolles area, though they are now exported to other parts of France. They produce the tenderest, leanest and best flavoured of beef. The pigs from the wilder parts of the region provide the tangy smoked Morvan hams. And then there are the plump, tasty chickens from Bresse, the only chickens that have an '*appelation controlée*', like a fine wine.

The Burgundian snails are the fattest of all, and the charcuterie shops are full of their pretty shells already plugged with garlic butter. The woods are full of game: venison, pheasant and woodcock, hare and wild rabbit. The rivers and streams offer ample crayfish, pike and trout.

Vegetables grow well in this fertile area, notably onions and carrots. *Nivernaise*, describing a dish, is enough to indicate that it is garnished with glazed carrots and onions, while *bourguignonne* usually indicates that diced bacon or smoked ham is also used with the carrots and onions, as well as red Burgundian wine. Mushrooms, and even truffles, are to be found, and fruit, especially pears and cherries, ripen in profusion.

Add to such natural endowment the skills developed over centuries, (you have only to look at the *Très Riches Heures* of the Duc de Berry to see the love of good things), and you have a cuisine that is rich and varied, but never over-elaborate. The great Burgundian dishes are not sophisticated restaurant productions. But such classics as *pouchouse*, the stew of freshwater fish, *boeuf bourguignonne*, *lapin à la moutarde*, *carottes Vichy* and *gougère*, are all dishes that belong to an area that has enjoyed centuries of prosperity and that has refined its cooking without ever losing the country origins of its cuisine.

There are also specialities associated with particular towns or districts. Dijon is of course world-famous for its mustards made with verjus, the juice of unripened grapes, but it also prides itself on its spiced honey cakes (*pain d'épices*) and the famous *jambon persillé*.

Wine is really the most important product of the area, and each region produces its own distinctive wine, which is the foundation of its wealth. No stay in Burgundy, however brief, is complete without at least a visit to the beautiful fifteenth-century Hotel Dieu at Beaune, still the site for one of the most important wine auctions of the year. Apart from wine, Burgundy also produces two marvellous drinks; first, *marc de bourgogne*, distilled from the residue of grapes after the pressing, a powerful but full-flavoured eau-de-vie, excellent for flavouring meat dishes or fruit salads, unless it is so mature that this would be sacrilege; and, secondly, *cassis*, one of the great specialities of the region, a liqueur distilled from blackcurrants, and invaluable for flavouring fruit desserts and ices, as well as making, with the addition of chilled white wine, the excellent and increasingly popular aperitif, *kir*.

Guyenne, Gascogne and Béarn

One of the most historic corners of France – it was here, in the Dordogne area of Guyenne, that Cro-Magnon man was found, and the prehistoric cave-paintings of Les Eyzies still astonish the visitor with their freshness and vigour – this is also an area of fine wines, rich food and pungent flavours.

There are delicious specialities all over the region. The long, straight Atlantic coastline provides tuna, squid and sardines, while oysters are farmed in the bay of Arcachon and are often eaten here, Spanish style, with spicy little sausages. The Basque influence is strong in this south-western corner of France, with tomatoes and peppers, especially the *piment basque* (almost, but not quite, as fiery as a chilli pepper) providing a dominant taste. The salt-cured hams of Bayonne, whose quality is still watched over by a 'brotherhood', have a strong individual character and are exported all over the world. This is also one of the first parts of France to be introduced to chocolate, brought by the Jews from Spain and Portugal in the sixteenth century, and it is still a chocolate-manufacturing area. The Béarn is the birthplace of Henri IV, the king whose pious wish it was that all his subjects should have a chicken in their pot on Sundays, and the *poule au pot Henri IV* is still something of a regional speciality though it has spread to other parts of France.

As you move a little further north, the woods provide wonderful mushrooms, especially *cèpes*, and ample and exotic game. Partridge, pheasant, woodcock, guineafowl, wild duck, wood pidgeon and ortolans appear on menus as frequently as hare, chicken, turkey and duck. But the goose is the national symbol of the Guyenne and the Gascogne, and strings of geese can be seen waddling down village streets and around every farmyard pond. Some are force-fed, to provide the huge distended livers for the *pâté de foie gras* for which the Perigord is world-famous. Goose is cooked a little differently wherever you go, according to local custom, but most often it is preserved in its own fat, and the *confit d'oie* adds a characteristic flavour to many dishes, such as the *garbure* of Béarn and the *cassoulet* of neighbouring Languedoc. Goosefat is used instead of butter in much of the local cooking, even sometimes for baking, and the famous *beurre de Gascogne* is none other than goose fat mixed with large quantities of mashed garlic.

There are other specialities: the town of Moissac has its chasselas grapes, sold in the market square outside its incomparably lovely romanesque church; walnuts grow in huge quantities around Sarlat; Agen is famous for its plums, mostly dried to make prunes, some of which are stuffed with a sweet liqueur-flavoured paste and sent around the world proudly proclaiming on their package '*je suis un pruneau d'Agen fourré*'. But of course the most important speciality of the Perigord is the truffle, that highly prized 'black diamond' which defies cultivation, and still needs trained pigs or dogs to snuffle it out, and which gives the *pâté de foie gras* of the Perigord its unique flavour, and, some would say, its supremacy over all other pâtés. Add to this the incomparable clarets from Bordeaux, Armagnac, the great brandy that is distilled in Gascony, the dessert wines from Monbazillac and the liqueurs from the Marie Brizard distilleries, and you have a gourmet's paradise.

Languedoc and Provence

These two Mediterranean provinces of France are like heavenly larders, so abundantly endowed are they by nature with glorious produce. The coastline provides the brilliantly coloured, weirdly shaped fish of the Mediterranean: seabass, known as 'wolf of the sea' (*loup de mer*), rosy mullet and silvery bream, fierce-looking rascasse and hideous gurnard, as well as sardines and shoals of anchovies. No wonder that the most famous dish from this part of France is the *bouillabaisse*, the great fish soup about whose precise correct contents aficionados argue interminably, the most fanatic among them claiming that the true *bouillabaisse* can only be obtained within sniffing distance of the port of Marseilles. Shellfish, from spiny lobsters (*langoustes*) and crabs, to clams, large and tiny, and sea-urchins, can also be enjoyed all along the coast, and especially in the restaurants and cafes of Sète and the little walled town of Aigues Mortes in the Camargue, that strange area of marshland, salt-pans, grey-blue skies, white horses and pink flamingos.

Provence has always had a magical quality, with its special light that has attracted painters as well as travellers, its groves of gnarled olive trees and its fragrant pinewoods which produce the pine kernels that are much used in Provençal cooking, its herb-covered slopes and its cornucopia of vivid vegetables and fruit. The big, puckered, deep orange tomatoes have a taste that lingers in the memory and makes other tomatoes seem pallid in comparison; the aubergines seem a deeper purple here than elsewhere; the fennel is fat, crisp and pungent, and the artichokes tiny, spiny and flushed with violet. The special, wide-stemmed spinach is used in sweet as well as savoury dishes, and the asparagus from Cavaillon is especially highly prized.

Cavaillon also produces some of the best melons – the astute Alexander Dumas once made a deal with the municipality of Cavaillon whereby he sent them a complete set of his more than four hundred works for their library in exchange for a life annuity of twelve Cavaillon melons a year, and hoped they found his books as charming as he found their fruit. The area around Carpentras and Avignon also grows wonderful peaches, pears, apricots, strawberries, cherries and even oranges and lemons, and nearby Apt has a flourishing glacé fruit industry. No wonder that the bees of Provence produce such fragrant honey.

Olive oil and garlic are the predominant flavours of the provençal cuisine, and fruit and vegetables its greatest glory. As you move westwards into the Languedoc, the cooking changes to a more solid, earthbound style. Pork products become more evident, chestnuts and walnuts take over from almonds, and pulses are used a great deal. The little green and grey lentils from Le Puy are especially delicious, and further south, Toulouse, Carcassonne and Castelnaudary vie with each other as to which produces the best *cassoulet*, that marvellously sustaining dish of meat and beans.

As you get closer to the Pyrenees, the influence of Spanish cooking makes itself felt; a paella cooked in Toulouse will be as good as any you come across in Spain.

The Languedoc is also the home of one of the world's great cheeses, the Roquefort, mentioned by Pliny, praised by Charlemagne and appreciated by Rabelais. It is made in the Aveyron area only, from the milk of ewes that have grazed on the herb-scented grass of those uplands, and then matured in the natural caves of Roquefort itself. It is the chief pride and glory of the Languedoc.

Auvergne, Lyonnais, Savoie and Dauphiné

The Auvergne is in the heart of the Massif Central, the great central mountainous area of France. It is the country of Vercingetorix and the Arverni, a war-like tribe, and it is still a wild and barren area, romantically beautiful for the traveller, but relatively poor, for the land is hard to cultivate. Not surprisingly, the food tends to be good and simple country fare rather than haute cuisine. Potatoes and cabbage are the most popular vegetables, and lentils from Le Puy, a little further South, are also in demand.

As with other mountainous areas, the Auvergne is noted for its hams, raw and cooked, and sausages, and you will find an unusual variety of pork products in the local charcuteries. But if one had to choose one single characteristic food from these high pastures, it would be cheese. Cantal, made from cow's milk, is the best known. It has a long lineage, being first mentioned by Pliny the Elder two thousand years ago. It is not unlike a Cheddar or Lancashire cheese, and, like these, it is equally good to eat plain or for use in cooking. Indeed, there is a *soupe de Cantal* that is so thick with bread and cheese that you can stand a spoon in it. But there are many other varieties of cheese – some made from goat's milk, others from the milk of ewes. The Bleu d'Auvergne is made by the same method as Roquefort, but, being made from cow's milk, is considerably less expensive.

As so often in mountainous districts, the puddings tend to be as substantial as the main dishes, but the area around Clermont-Ferrand is a fertile fruit-growing valley, where there are not only a great many apple orchards, but cherries, apricots, strawberries and above all angelica are grown. This is a great centre for making glacé fruits and fruit pastes, while nearby Royat has a flourishing chocolate industry.

The Lyonnais is an altogether more prosperous region, and the Lyonnaises regard their city as the centre of French gastronomy; certainly the area boasts an uncommon number of starred restaurants. Although a small region, it is blessed with the products of its neighbours – Burgundy is not far away, with its fine wines, its Charollais beef and chickens from Bresse. The fertile Rhône valley produces fruit and vegetables, notably onions, which are used so extensively in Lyonnaise cooking that the word on a menu is enough to imply that the dish contains onions. The truffles found in the area, while not as highly prized as those from the Perigord, are used in regional dishes, especially the famous *poulet demi-deuil*. Thin slices of truffle are slipped under the skin of the chicken breast before it is poached, giving it the appearance of being in half-mourning – a characteristically elaborate speciality of Lyons, and invented by the great Mère Fillioux, doyenne of Lyon's formidable army of women restaurateurs.

The Savoie and Dauphiné share borders along the Alps with Switzerland and Italy. This is an area of high mountains with inviting valleys, lakes and streams, and the cooking is simple, relying on the quality of the ingredients for its effects. There are fresh fish from the lakes and streams – carp, eel, pike and crayfish; the romantically named *omble chevalier*, a kind of char, may be eaten here.

Cheeses are one of the chief products from the high alpine pastures, especially the dense Beaufort, used in fondue, and Reblochon, made near beautiful Lake Annecy.

The Dauphiné is also the home of Chartreuse, made to a sixteenth-century recipe from 130 aromatic plants and herbs that grow on the wooded slopes of the area.

Further south, in the Bas-Dauphiné, lies the town of Montélimar, devoted to the manufacture of nougat, made with almonds that have been grown in the area since almond trees were first planted there in the sixteenth century, and with the fragrant honey from Provence.

Soups

Potage Aux Moules *Mussel Soup*

BRITTANY

Mussels abound around the flat marshy Northern coastline of Brittany, and are served in numerous different ways, some more extravagant than others. This simple soup would be served piping hot from a fat tureen to start the family evening meal.

Preparation time: 20 minutes (plus cleaning mussels)
Cooking time: 15 minutes
To serve: 6

1 litre/1¾ pints mussels, cleaned
150 ml/¼ pint white wine or cider
50 g/2 oz butter
25 g/1 oz flour
1 litre/1¾ pints hot milk
pinch of cayenne
salt
freshly ground black pepper
pinch of saffron powder
2 tablespoons crème fraîche (see page 118) or double cream
1 egg yolk
1 tablespoon finely chopped fresh parsley

Put the mussels in a large saucepan with the wine or cider, cover the pan and cook over a high heat until the mussels open. Remove the mussels with a slotted spoon as soon as they open and take the meat from the shells. Discard any that do not open. Keep warm. Strain the liquid and reserve.

In a clean saucepan melt the butter, stir in the flour and cook over a gentle heat, without allowing to colour, for 3 minutes. Remove from the heat and gradually stir in the strained mussel liquid. Stir until smooth, then slowly add the hot milk. Return to the heat and bring the soup to the boil. Stir in the cayenne, and salt and pepper to taste.

Mix the saffron and the crème fraîche with the egg yolk and add a little of the hot soup. Stir until smooth, then add to the rest of the soup together with the mussels. Heat through without allowing to boil. Sprinkle with the parsley before serving.

Potage Vert A La Crème *Cream of Artichoke Soup*

BRITTANY

Although globe artichokes grow to such fat and meaty perfection in the north of Brittany, you will rarely find them served here with the delicate sauces with which they appear in the richer parts of France. They may be served as an hors d'oeuvre with a simple vinaigrette, but more often they are used to flavour dishes such as this delicate and subtle soup.

Preparation time: 30 minutes
Cooking time: 30 minutes
To serve: 6 to 8

2 large globe artichokes
salt
50 g/2 oz butter
2 potatoes, peeled and cubed
2 leeks, white parts only, thinly sliced
1 lettuce, leaves separated
1.5 litres/2½ pints stock or water
1 egg yolk
150 ml/¼ pint crème fraîche (see page 118)
freshly ground black pepper

Trim the stalk off the artichokes and trim the leaves right down, using kitchen scissors. Plunge the artichokes into boiling salted water and cook until just tender. Drain. When cool enough to handle, remove the leaves and hairy choke. Roughly chop the hearts.

Melt the butter in a large saucepan, add the potatoes and leeks, cover and cook gently for 5 minutes to soften. Add the lettuce leaves and the chopped artichoke hearts. Stir in the stock or water. Bring to the boil and simmer for 20 minutes or until all the vegetables are quite tender.

Pass the soup through a blender or mouli-légumes, and then through a nylon sieve to remove any fibres. Return to a clean pan and bring back to the boil.

Mix the egg yolk with the crème fraîche. Take the soup off the heat and add the cream mixture. Return to the heat and heat through without allowing to boil, stirring well. Add salt and pepper to taste and serve.

Soupe A La Bretonne *Haricot Bean Soup*

BRITTANY

A really filling farmhouse soup. Serve it on a cold day.

Preparation time: 15 minutes (plus soaking overnight)
Cooking time: 1 to 3 hours
To serve: 6 to 8

225 g/8 oz dried haricot beans, soaked in water overnight
50 g/2 oz butter
2 onions, finely chopped
2 leeks, white parts only, thinly sliced
2 large tomatoes, skinned and chopped
2 litres/3½ pints stock, or water and a good stock bone
1 bouquet garni (bay leaf and thyme and rosemary sprigs)
salt
freshly ground black pepper
1 tablespoon finely chopped fresh parsley

Drain and rinse the beans. Put them in a saucepan, cover with fresh cold water and bring to the boil. Drain and rinse again.

Melt half the butter in a large saucepan, add the onions and leeks and fry over a gentle heat until softened. Add the tomatoes and beans, then add the stock, or the water and bone, and the bouquet garni. Bring to the boil, then cover and simmer for at least 1 hour or until the beans are tender. If they are not fresh, they may take considerably longer to cook.

When the beans are quite soft, remove the bouquet garni and bone, if used, and pass the soup through a blender or mouli-légumes. Return the soup to the pan and reheat gently. Add salt and pepper, then stir in the remaining butter, cut into small pieces, to give the soup a glaze. Sprinkle with the parsley and serve.

Potage vert a la crème and potage aux moules

Crème Dieppoise *Cream of Fish and Mussel Soup*

NORMANDY

This soup is almost a meal in itself, and though it is rich, and requires several processes to make, it is not expensive and is well worth the effort. White fish, such as cod is excellent. Serve with crusty French bread, and follow with a light omelette or salad.

Preparation time: 40 minutes (plus cleaning mussels)
Cooking time: 50 minutes
To serve: 6 to 8

0.5 kg/1 lb filleted white fish, and about 225 g/8 oz of the fish bones, heads or trimmings reserved
dash of wine vinegar
1 litre/1$\frac{3}{4}$ pints mussels, cleaned
300 ml/$\frac{1}{2}$ pint wine or cider
75 g/3 oz butter
2 onions, finely chopped
1 carrot, finely chopped
2 large leeks, white parts only, finely chopped
2 celery sticks, finely chopped
100 g/4 oz white mushrooms, finely chopped
1 tablespoon flour
1 bay leaf
1 parsley sprig
salt
freshly ground black pepper
150 ml/$\frac{1}{4}$ pint crème fraîche (see page 118)
1 egg yolk
1 tablespoon finely chopped fresh parsley

Put the fish bones and trimmings in a saucepan, add the vinegar and cover with cold water. Bring to the boil and simmer for 20 minutes. Strain the stock and make it up to 1 litre/1$\frac{3}{4}$ pints with water.

Put the mussels in a large saucepan with the wine or cider, cover the pan and cook over a high heat until the mussels open. Remove the mussels with a slotted spoon as soon as they open, take the meat from the shells and set aside. Discard any mussels that remain closed. Strain the cooking liquid and reserve.

Melt 50 g/2 oz of the butter in a large saucepan, add the vegetables and cook gently until they are soft, but not browned. Sprinkle with the flour, stir well and continue to cook over a low heat for 3 minutes, without allowing to brown.

Add the fish, fish stock, bay leaf and parsley and bring to the boil, stirring well. Cover and simmer for 5 to 10 minutes or until the fish is tender.

Remove the bay leaf and parsley, then blend or pass through a mouli-légumes. Return the soup to a clean saucepan and stir in the cooking liquid from the mussels and salt and pepper to taste. Bring to the boil. Remove from the heat and stir in the crème fraîche mixed with the egg yolk, followed by the mussels and the remaining butter cut into small pieces. Heat through gently without allowing to boil. Sprinkle with the parsley and serve.

Potage Crécy *Carrot Soup*

ILE-DE-FRANCE

Some of the best carrots come from the area around Crécy, east of Paris, so this light and delicately coloured soup takes its name from there.

Preparation time: 20 minutes
Cooking time: 30 to 40 minutes
To serve: 6

100 g/4 oz butter
0.5 kg/1 lb carrots, sliced
1 medium onion, finely chopped
$\frac{1}{2}$ teaspoon sugar
salt
freshly ground black pepper
50 g/2 oz long-grain rice
900 ml/1$\frac{1}{2}$ pints hot chicken or veal stock
2 parsley sprigs
2 slices of stale white bread, cubed

Melt half the butter in a heavy saucepan and add the carrots, onion, sugar and salt and pepper to taste. Cover and sweat over a gentle heat for 10 minutes.

Add the rice and stir well, then pour on the hot stock. Add the parsley sprigs. Bring to the boil, cover and simmer for 20 minutes, or until the vegetables and the rice are quite soft.

Remove the parsley sprigs and pass the soup through a blender or mouli-légumes, and then through a nylon sieve. Return to a clean saucepan, adjust the seasoning and heat through.

Melt 40 g/1$\frac{1}{2}$ oz of the remaining butter in a frying pan and fry the cubes of bread until they are crisp and golden brown. Drain on paper towels.

Cut the remaining butter into small pieces, add to the soup to give it a glaze. Serve very hot, with the croûtons served separately.

Potage Normande Fish Soup with Prawns

NORMANDY

This soup looks deceptively bland but it has a richly fishy flavour.

Preparation time: 25 minutes
Cooking time: 20 minutes
To serve: 6

600 ml/1 pint cooked prawns in their shells
225 g/8 oz filleted fish, bones reserved
150 ml/$\frac{1}{4}$ pint white wine or cider
1 litre/1$\frac{3}{4}$ pints water
1 bouquet garni
25 g/1 oz butter
1 onion, finely chopped
1 carrot, finely chopped
1 celery stick, finely chopped
50 g/2 oz fresh white breadcrumbs
salt
freshly ground black pepper
pinch of saffron powder
juice of $\frac{1}{2}$ lemon or to taste
150 ml/$\frac{1}{4}$ pint crème fraîche (see page 118)
1 egg yolk
1 tablespoon finely chopped fresh parsley

Peel the prawns, reserving the shells. Put the fish bones and prawn shells into a saucepan, add the wine or cider, water and bouquet garni and bring to the boil. Simmer for 20 minutes. Strain the stock.

Melt the butter in a large saucepan, add the vegetables and cook without stirring for 5 minutes. Add the fish and cook very gently until tender.

Put the fish mixture, prawns and breadcrumbs into a blender or food processor together with a little of the fish stock and blend until smooth. Return to the saucepan and add the remaining fish stock, saffron, lemon juice and salt and pepper to taste. Bring to the boil, stirring occasionally. Stir in the crème fraîche mixed with the egg yolk and heat through without allowing to boil. Adjust the seasoning, sprinkle with the parsley and serve.

Soupe A L'Oignon Onion Soup

PARIS

One of the best known of French soups, this used to be served, piping hot and well laced with Cognac, in the early hours of the morning in Les Halles, when this was still the central market of Paris. Though the soup itself is quite thin, it is warming and very sustaining. The cheese croûte gradually gets softened and impregnated with the soup as you pull it down into the bowl to cut off a piece with each spoonful.

Preparation time: 30 minutes
Cooking time: 45 minutes
To serve: 6

50 g/2 oz butter
1 tablespoon oil
0.5 kg/1 lb onions, thinly sliced
$\frac{1}{2}$ teaspoon sugar
1 tablespoon flour
1 litre/1$\frac{3}{4}$ pints beef stock
salt
freshly ground black pepper
6 slices of stale French bread
1 garlic clove, halved
100 g/4 oz Gruyère cheese, grated
2 tablespoons brandy (optional)

Melt the butter with the oil in a large heavy saucepan and add the onions. Stir well. Cover and cook over a moderate heat for 20 minutes, or until the onions are quite soft and butter yellow. Raise the heat, sprinkle on the sugar and cook, uncovered and stirring frequently, until the onions turn a rich golden brown.

Sprinkle with the flour and when this has also browned, add the stock and salt and pepper to taste. Stir well. Bring to the boil, cover and simmer for another 20 minutes.

Meanwhile, rub the slices of bread with the cut surface of the clove of garlic. Dry or toast gently under a moderate grill. Pile a little of the cheese on each slice and melt under the grill until lightly browned.

When the soup is ready, adjust the seasoning and add the brandy, if used. Pour into individual bowls and float a cheese croûte in each bowl.

La Potée *Bacon and Vegetable Soup*

PICARDY

A cross between a soup and a hot-pot, rather like a pot-au-feu, this is a real peasant dish, which can be eaten all in one, or served in two courses, with the broth followed by the meat and vegetables. The vegetable ingredients do not have to be exact, and the country housewife would simply use whatever vegetables are at hand.

Preparation time: 15 minutes
Cooking time: about 2 hours
To serve: 6 to 8

about 1 kg/2 lb piece of bacon, soaked overnight if very salty and drained
2 leeks
1 bouquet garni
6 to 8 carrots, peeled or scraped
6 to 8 medium potatoes, peeled
6 to 8 small onions, peeled
1 small cabbage, quartered, cored, blanched and shredded
225 g/8 oz shelled peas or broad beans
salt
freshly ground black pepper
2 to 3 slices of thick wholemeal bread (optional)

Put the bacon into a very large saucepan or stewpot, cover with fresh water and bring to the boil. Boil gently for 10 minutes, then throw away the water.

Rinse the bacon and the stewpot and cover again with at least $2\frac{1}{4}$ litres/4 pints cold water. Bring to the boil, add the leeks and bouquet garni and simmer for 1 hour. Add the carrots, potatoes and onions and simmer for a further 30 minutes.

Remove the leeks and the bouquet garni. Add the cabbage and peas or beans and simmer for another 10 to 15 minutes, or until the green vegetables are cooked.

Remove the piece of bacon to a heated serving dish, and surround with the vegetables.

Taste the broth for seasoning; add a little salt if necessary and some pepper. If the soup is to be served separately, it is often poured onto some thick slices of wholemeal bread for serving.

Soupe à la citrouille and la potée

Soupe A La Citrouille *Pumpkin Soup*

PICARDY

If you are making a large quantity of this soup, the prettiest way to serve it is to use a whole or a half pumpkin. Hollow out the pumpkin carefully, and serve the soup in the shell.

Preparation time: 15 minutes
Cooking time: 20 minutes
To serve: 6

1 kg/2 lb pumpkin, peeled, seeded and cubed
1 onion, peeled
3 cloves
1 litre/1¾ pints milk
600 ml/1 pint stock or water
1 bay leaf
salt
freshly ground black pepper
50 g/2 oz butter
1 thick slice of stale white bread, cubed
1 tablespoon crème fraîche (see page 118), (optional)

Put the pumpkin cubes into a large saucepan with the onion stuck with the cloves, the milk, stock or water, bay leaf and salt and pepper to taste. Bring to the boil and simmer until the pumpkin is very tender.

Remove the cloves and bay leaf. Put the soup through a blender or mouli-légumes and then through a fine sieve. Return to the clean saucepan, reheat and adjust the seasoning.

Meanwhile melt all but 15 g/½ oz of the butter in a frying pan. When foaming add the cubes of bread and fry until golden brown on all sides. Drain on paper towels.

Stir the reserved butter into the soup to give it a glaze, swirl in the crème fraiche, if used, and scatter on the croûtons just before serving.

La Chaudrée Charentaise *Fish Chowder*

CHARENTE

The American word 'chowder' derives from the *chaudrées* of the Atlantic coast of France, where fish soups or stews are cooked in tall *chaudrons* or cauldrons. An assortment of sea fish, such as sole, hake, plaice, flounder, cod or whiting would be used, as well as eel and cuttlefish and even sometimes carp.

Preparation time: 20 minutes
Cooking time: 35 to 40 minutes
To serve: 6

100 g/4 oz butter
12 small onions, peeled
12 medium potatoes, peeled
salt
freshly ground black pepper
1 kg/2 to 2¼ lb assorted firm fish (see above), cleaned and cut into large chunks or filleted
1 bouquet garni
1 litre/1¾ pints white wine
6 slices of stale white bread
1 garlic clove, halved
1 tablespoon oil
1 tablespoon finely chopped fresh parsley

Melt 25 g/1 oz of the butter in a heavy flameproof casserole or cauldron. Put in the onions, lay the potatoes on top, dot them with another 25 g/1 oz of the butter and season generously with salt and pepper. Lay the fish on top of the potatoes, starting with the firmest fish and ending with the softest. Put the bouquet garni on top.

Bring the wine to the boil in a separate saucepan and pour into the casserole. Cover and simmer for about 30 minutes.

Meanwhile, rub the slices of bread on both sides with the cut surface of the clove of garlic. Melt half the remaining butter with the oil in a frying pan and quickly fry the bread until it is golden brown on both sides. Drain on paper towels.

Remove the pieces of fish to a heated serving tureen as they are cooked, and keep warm. When all the fish and the potatoes are done and have been transferred to the tureen, raise the heat and bring the liquid to the boil. Boil fiercely to reduce for 5 minutes.

Remove from the heat, add the remaining butter cut into small pieces and pour into the tureen. Sprinkle with the parsley and serve hot.

Serve the fried bread separately, allowing everyone to put a slice into their plates before adding the soup.

Soupe A La Savoyarde Celeriac Soup

SAVOIE

A sustaining soup, this has a very subtle flavour.

Preparation time: 10 minutes
Cooking time: 30 minutes
To serve: 6

50 g/2 oz butter
1 large celeriac (about 350 g/12 oz), peeled and diced
1 onion, finely chopped
1 large potato, peeled and diced
900 ml/1½ pints chicken stock
salt
freshly ground black pepper
300 ml/½ pint milk
1 tablespoon finely chopped fresh parsley

Melt the butter in a large heavy saucepan, add the vegetables, cover and cook very gently for 10 minutes to soften, without allowing them to brown.

Add the stock and salt and pepper to taste and bring to the boil. Simmer until the vegetables are tender. Put through a blender or mouli-légumes and return to the clean saucepan.

Stir in the milk and bring to the boil. Adjust the seasoning, adding plenty of pepper to counteract the slight sweetness of the celeriac. Sprinkle with the parsley before serving.

Potée Au Chou Savoyarde Pork and Vegetable Soup

SAVOIE

More like a hotpot than a soup, this is a meal in itself, economical and satisfying.

Preparation time: 20 minutes
Cooking time: 2½ hours
To serve: 6 to 8

50 g/2 oz lard
0.5 kg/1 lb lean pork
225 g/8 oz salt pork, soaked in cold water overnight
0.5 kg/1 lb carrots, halved or quartered
2 leeks, finely chopped
0.5 kg/1 lb turnips, peeled if necessary and halved
1 bouquet garni
2 garlic cloves, peeled
4 cloves
0.75 kg/1½ lb potatoes, peeled and halved or quartered
2 onions, quartered
1 large boiling sausage
1 savoy cabbage, quartered and cored
salt
freshly ground black pepper

Melt the lard in a very large saucepan and quickly brown both pieces of pork on all sides. Add the carrots, leeks and turnips, cover with cold water and add the bouquet garni and the cloves of garlic stuck with the cloves. Bring slowly to the boil. Simmer for about 1 hour.

Add the potatoes, onions and the sausage, well-pricked with a fork, and continue to simmer for another hour.

Blanch the cabbage in boiling salted water for 2 minutes, then drain and add to the pot. Simmer for a further 30 minutes.

Adjust the seasoning and remove the bouquet garni before serving.

La Garbure Béarnaise *Vegetable and Meat Soup*

BEARN

An age-old country soup, this is a hefty meal in itself. It belongs to the mountainous region of the Pyrenees, where the weather can be very raw, and goose, and especially goose fat, is used a good deal to provide internal insulation. When this is not available, pork and pork fat may be used instead. The custom of *faire chabrol* is associated with this soup – a glass of wine is added to the remaining broth in each plate after all the meat and vegetables have been eaten.

Preparation time: 40 minutes
Cooking time: $2\frac{1}{2}$ hours
To serve: 8 minimum

225 g/8 oz bacon in the piece
1 piece preserved goose, or *225 g/8 oz smoked pork in the piece*
1 celery stick
6 garlic cloves, lightly crushed
1 large onion, peeled
2 cloves
1 bouquet garni
salt
freshly ground black pepper
4 large potatoes, peeled and cubed
1 turnip, diced
2 leeks, sliced
4 carrots, diced
225 g/8 oz shelled broad beans
225 g/8 oz shelled peas
1 small cabbage, cored and shredded
8 slices of strong country bread

Put the pieces of bacon and goose or pork into a very large saucepan and sweat gently until the fat begins to run. Remove the piece of goose, but leave the pork.

Add the celery, garlic, the onion stuck with the cloves and the bouquet garni and cover with as much cold water as the saucepan will hold ($3\frac{1}{2}$ litres/6 pints would not be too much, but add as much as you can and top up when possible during the cooking time). Season liberally and bring slowly to the boil. Keep at a steady simmer for 30 minutes, then add the potatoes, turnip, leeks and carrots and cook for another hour.

Add the beans and peas. When the soup has simmered for another 30 minutes add the cabbage and return the goose, if used, to the pot. Cook for at least a further 30 minutes.

Take out the pieces of meat and cut into chunks. Return these to the pot. Adjust the seasoning. Put a slice of bread in each soup plate and pour the soup over to serve.

Potage Purée Des Petits Pois Frais St. Germain

Smooth Green Pea Soup St. Germain style

ILE DE FRANCE

St Germain is the student quarter of Paris, the famous 'Left Bank'. But this delicate, elegant soup is more at home in the salons of the well-off intellectuals of the precinct.

Preparation time: 30 minutes
Cooking time: 30 minutes
To serve: 6

0.5 kg/1 lb shelled green peas
salt
50 g/2 oz butter
1.5 litres/$2\frac{1}{2}$ pints chicken stock
150 ml/$\frac{1}{4}$ pint double cream
chopped fresh chervil to garnish

Shell approximately 1 kg/2 lb of peas to obtain 500 g/1 lb shelled green peas. Cook them in the minimum of boiling salted water for 10–15 minutes until tender. Drain and reserve 2 tablespoons of the peas. Return the remainder to a large saucepan and sauté gently in the butter for a few minutes. Add the chicken stock and bring to the boil. Lower the heat and simmer for 10 minutes.

Remove the saucepan from the heat, and put the soup a little at a time through a blender or mouli légumes. Return the pea purée to the saucepan and simmer, while adding the cream. Sprinkle with the reserved peas and cook for 1 minute. Serve the soup in heated bowls and scatter chopped chervil on top.

Crème Vichyssoise *Leek and Potato Soup*

BOURBONNAIS

This delicate and pretty summer soup takes its name from the elegant spa town of Vichy which was the home of its inventor. It is a relative newcomer and does not really belong to traditional French cooking, but it is too good to omit.

Preparation time: 20 minutes
Cooking time: 20 minutes
To serve: 4 to 6

25 g/1 oz butter
1 kg/2 lb leeks, white parts only, chopped
225 g/8 oz potatoes, peeled and diced
1 litre/1¾ pints chicken or veal stock
salt
white pepper
300 ml/½ pint single cream
2 tablespoons chopped fresh chives

Melt the butter in a large saucepan, add the leeks and potatoes and soften, stirring well so that they become evenly coated with butter. Add the stock and salt and pepper to taste, bring to the boil and simmer until the vegetables are quite tender.

Put through a blender or mouli-légumes until smooth and chill.

Just before serving, stir in the cream, adjust the seasoning and sprinkle with the chopped chives.

Soupe A L'Oseille *Sorrel Soup*

BURGUNDY

Sorrel, with its long red stalks and pointed green acid leaves, grows wild in many country districts in central France, as well as in kitchen gardens, and makes this lovely light and simple refreshing soup.

Preparation time: 10 minutes
Cooking time: 15 minutes
To serve: 6

50 g/2 oz butter
1 large onion, finely chopped
1 potato, peeled and diced
225 g/8 oz sorrel leaves, stripped off the thicker stalks
1.5 litres/2½ pints chicken stock
salt
freshly ground black pepper
150 ml/¼ pint cream
2 egg yolks

Melt 40 g/1½ oz of the butter in a large heavy saucepan, add the onion and potato and fry until the onion is softened. Add the sorrel leaves and cook, stirring, over a moderate heat for a few minutes until the sorrel has wilted. Add the stock and cook for a further 5 minutes. Season to taste with salt and pepper.

Stir the cream into the egg yolks to make a smooth mixture, then add a little of the soup and stir until smooth. Add to the remaining soup and heat, stirring, over a moderate heat; do not allow to boil. Adjust the seasoning and add the remaining butter, a little at a time, to give the soup a glaze. Serve hot.

Soupe à l'oseille, crème Vichyssoise and soupe aux mousserons

Soupe Aux Mousserons *Mushroom Soup*

BURGUNDY

Made with full-flavoured field mushrooms, or *mousserons des près*, this is a fine soup, light but with a full flavour. If cultivated mushrooms have to be used, double the quantity.

Preparation time: 15 minutes
Cooking time: 30 minutes
To serve: 4 to 6

50 g/2 oz butter
1 onion, finely chopped
225 g/8 oz mushrooms, roughly chopped
1 tablespoon flour
1.5 litres/2½ pints hot chicken or veal stock
4 slices of French bread
50 g/2 oz Gruyère or Comté cheese, finely grated
salt
freshly ground black pepper
pinch of grated nutmeg
2 tablespoons crème fraiche (see page 118) or single cream
1 tablespoon chopped fresh parsley

Melt the butter in a large heavy saucepan, add the onion and fry until lightly coloured. Add the mushrooms and cook just until they begin to give out their moisture. Sprinkle on the flour and cook, stirring, for 2 minutes, without allowing to brown. Stir in the stock until smooth. Bring to the boil, then simmer for 15 minutes.

Meanwhile, toast the slices of bread lightly and put them in the bottom of a heated soup tureen. Sprinkle with the cheese and keep warm.

Blend the soup very briefly – it should not be completely smooth but should be quite a thin soup with small pieces of mushrooms in it. Reheat and season to taste with salt and pepper and the nutmeg. Bring just to the boil, then pour over the bread in the tureen and leave to soak for a few minutes.

Add a swirl of cream and sprinkle with parsley before serving.

Soupe Gratinée Lyonnaise *Cheese and Onion Soup*

LYONNAIS

The Auvergne has a *soupe de Cantal*, an onion and cheese soup which is so dense that you can stand a spoon in it. This is a lighter version, to be made with Cantal or Gruyère cheese.

Preparation time: 20 minutes
Cooking time: 1 hour
Oven temperature: 220°C, 425°F, Gas Mark 7
To serve: 6

100 g/4 oz butter
0.5 kg/1 lb onions, finely chopped
25 g/1 oz flour
pinch of dried mixed herbs
salt
freshly ground black pepper
1 litre/1¾ pints water
6 slices of French bread
175 g/6 oz Cantal or Gruyère cheese, grated
2 egg yolks
1 tablespoon brandy or marc

Melt the butter in a large heavy saucepan and add the onions. Cover and cook over a moderate heat until the onions are almost melted and golden yellow. They must not be allowed to brown.

Sprinkle on the flour, stir well and cook for a further 2 minutes. Add the herbs and salt and pepper to taste, then slowly stir in the water. Bring to the boil, cover and simmer for at least 30 minutes. Put the soup through a blender or mouli-légumes and adjust the seasoning.

Dry out the pieces of bread in the oven or toast them quite lightly. Place them in an ovenproof tureen, sprinkle on half the cheese and pour on the soup. Sprinkle the remaining cheese on top. Place the tureen in the oven and heat for 10 to 15 minutes or until the cheese has melted and begins to form a crust.

Whisk the egg yolks with the brandy or marc and pour into the soup. Give a good stir and serve very hot.

Soupe Au Lait Aux Oignons *Onion and Milk Soup*

LORRAINE

This is a really warming and sustaining, but delicately flavoured soup.

Preparation time: 15 minutes
Cooking time: 40 minutes
To serve: 6 to 8

100 g/4 oz butter
0.5 kg/1 lb onions, finely chopped
salt
freshly ground black pepper
good pinch of grated nutmeg
600 ml/1 pint chicken stock
900 ml/1½ pints milk
4 slices of stale white bread, cubed
1 egg yolk
2 tablespoons crème fraîche (see page 118) or double cream

Melt half the butter in a large, heavy saucepan and add the onions. Season with salt, pepper and nutmeg, cover and soften for about 10 minutes, without allowing the onions to brown. They should be a rich buttery yellow.

Add the chicken stock, bring to the boil and simmer, uncovered, for 20 minutes, so that the stock becomes reduced to half its original quantity.

Pass the soup through a blender or mouli-légumes. If the onions have been very finely chopped, you may wish to omit this step. Return to the saucepan, add the milk and simmer for another 10 minutes.

Melt the remaining butter in a frying pan and quickly fry the bread cubes until they are golden brown. Drain on paper towels.

Stir the egg yolk and cream together. Add a little of the soup and stir to make a smooth sauce. Pour into the remaining soup, stir well and adjust the seasoning. Serve the soup very hot, adding the croûtons of bread at the last minute.

Hors d'Oeuvres, Pâtés and Salads

Galantine De Canard

Duck Pâté
NORMANDY

The *charcuteries* of Rouen are a delight and their windows as enticing to the eye as a toyshop. There are rabbit pâtés moulded into rabbit shapes, and duck pâtés moulded into ducks, as well as a wonderful selection of terrines in casseroles shaped as nesting pheasants, venison rampant, and rabbits couchant. This duck pâté, though it requires some skill in boning the duck – or a butcher willing to do it for you – is not difficult to make, and is rich and delicious as well as looking impressive. Keep the carcass for stock.

Preparation time: about 40 minutes (plus marinating and setting)
Cooking time: $1\frac{1}{2}$ hours
Oven temperature: 180°C, 350°F, Gas Mark 4
To serve: 10 to 12

1 oven-ready duck, boned, giblets reserved
2 to 3 extra duck or chicken livers (optional)
2 to 3 shallots, halved
strip of orange rind
pinch of ground allspice
1 fresh thyme branch
2 bay leaves
salt
freshly ground black pepper
3 tablespoons Calvados
25 g/1 oz butter
6 to 8 shallots, finely chopped
225 g/8 oz lean pork, minced
225 g/8 oz pork fat, minced
225 g/8 oz veal, minced
1 egg
3 to 4 strips of pork fat or streaky bacon

Galantine de canard

Cut off as much meat from the duck after boning as is possible without damaging the skin. Cut the meat into strips and place in a bowl. Add the giblet meat and livers, also cut into large strips, the halved shallots, orange rind, allspice, thyme, 1 bay leaf and salt and pepper to taste. Sprinkle on the Calvados and leave to marinate overnight, or at least for a few hours. Strain off the marinading liquid and reserve.

Melt the butter in a frying pan, add the chopped shallots and cook until golden brown. Combine the minced meats well in a bowl and add the cooked shallots and the egg beaten with the strained marinading liquid. Mix well together and add salt and pepper to taste. (It is worth cooking a small pat of the forcemeat in a little butter to get the seasoning right.)

Spread the duck skin flat on a working surface, outside down. Put half the forcemeat into the centre and flatten the surface. Make a layer of the duck meat and liver mixture on top and cover with remaining forcemeat. Pat into a good rounded shape. Wrap the sides of the duck skin right around and sew it up, first down the centre and then all the other openings.

Season the outside of the duck parcel lightly and place in an oval terrine of the right size. Cover the top with the second bay leaf and the strips of pork fat or bacon. Cook in the oven for $1\frac{1}{2}$ hours, or until the juice that comes out, when the pâté is pricked with a skewer, is just clear.

Place a piece of buttered greaseproof or wax paper, butter side down, over the pâté, put a board on top and then add a heavy weight to press the pâté down. Leave overnight to set and to allow the flavour to mature. You can serve the galantine from the terrine, or you may unmould it before serving.

Hors D'Oeuvre Aux Crevettes

Shrimp Appetizer
NORMANDY

A substantial and refreshing hors d'oeuvre, this can be made with shrimps or prawns.

Preparation time: 15 minutes
To serve: 4

1 small lettuce, leaves separated
2 eating apples, cored and chopped
100 g/4 oz shrimps or prawns, peeled
100 g/4 oz walnuts, roughly chopped
good squeeze of lemon juice
salt and freshly ground black pepper
½ teaspoon French mustard
2 tablespoons crème fraîche (see page 118) or double cream

Line a salad bowl with the lettuce leaves. In another bowl, mix together the apples, shrimps or prawns and walnuts and sprinkle with the lemon juice. Season to taste with salt and pepper. Stir the mustard into the crème fraîche, season again and fold into the apple, shrimp and walnut mixture. Spoon into the centre of the salad bowl and serve.

Hors d'oeuvre aux crevettes

Omelette Poularde *Soufflé Omelette*

NORMANDY

This is a speciality of La Mère Poularde, proprietor of the famous restaurant that nestles at the foot of Mont St Michel. There the omelette is served between the fish and meat course, but it may well be served as a simple lunch or supper dish.
Fresh eggs are essential for this dish.

Preparation time: 5 minutes
Cooking time: 5 to 8 minutes
To serve: 1

2 fresh eggs, separated
salt
freshly ground black pepper
15 g/½ oz butter

Beat the egg yolks lightly with salt and pepper to taste. Beat the whites until they stand in peaks but are not quite dry. Fold them into the yolks. Heat the omelette pan over a high heat, then lower the heat and put in the butter. Swirl the butter round the pan. When the butter is sizzling but has not changed colour, pour in the omelette mixture.

Shake the pan a little, and as the omelette begins to set, scrape the bottom of the pan gently with a fork, and run a palette knife round the edges. As soon as the bottom of the omelette has become golden brown and slightly crisp, slip the palette knife underneath and fold the omelette in half. Slide onto a heated plate and serve.

Salade Cauchoise *Potato, Celery and Ham Salad*

NORMANDY

A nourishing salad, serve it for lunch or after a light main course.

Preparation time: 10 minutes
Cooking time: 15 minutes
To serve: 4

0.5 kg/1 lb new or waxy potatoes
1 large head of celery, trimmed and cut into thin strips
salt
freshly ground black pepper
2 tablespoons wine vinegar
200 ml/⅓ pint crème fraîche (see page 118)
100 g/4 oz cooked ham, cut into thin strips
½ tablespoon finely chopped fresh parsley

Cook the potatoes in their skins in boiling water until just tender. Drain, then peel while still hot. Cut into thin strips. Mix the celery gently with the potato and season generously with salt and pepper. Sprinkle on the vinegar and cool.

Whip the cream lightly and fold into the potato mixture. Sprinkle with the ham and parsley and serve.

Salade Aux Moules *Mussel Salad*

ARTOIS

A tasty fish salad, serve this as a rather substantial hors d'oeuvre.

Preparation time: 20 minutes (plus cleaning of mussels)
Cooking time: 30 minutes
To serve: 6

2 litres/3½ pints mussels, cleaned
150 ml/¼ pint white wine
1 small onion, finely chopped
1 bouquet garni
0.5 kg/1 lb new potatoes
1 quantity sauce vinaigrette (see page 110)
1 tablespoon chopped fresh chives

Put the mussels in a large saucepan with the wine, onion and bouquet garni. Cover the pan and cook over a high heat until the mussels open, shaking the pan from time to time so that the mussels cook evenly. Remove the mussels with a slotted spoon as soon as they open, take the meat from the shells and set aside. Discard any mussels that remain closed. Strain the cooking liquid and reserve.

Cook the potatoes in their skins in boiling water until just tender. Drain and, as soon as they are cool enough to handle, peel and slice them quickly. Sprinkle 2 or 3 tablespoons of the strained mussel liquid over the potatoes, stir in the vinaigrette, add the mussels and turn well. Leave to cool.

Sprinkle with the chives before serving.

Les Betteraves Au Four *Baked Beetroot*

PICARDY

Beetroot are mostly served hot, and usually on their own, so that their colour does not contaminate other food, and their full flavour, which is beautifully preserved by this cooking method, can be appreciated. Use small young beetroot, very fresh.

Preparation time: 10 minutes
Cooking time: 45 minutes to 1 hour
Oven temperature: 190°C, 375°F, Gas Mark 5
To serve: 4

0.5 kg/1 lb beetroot
15 g/½ oz butter
squeeze of lemon juice
salt
freshly ground black pepper

Wash the beetroot but do not peel them. Cut the stalk off well above the root, to prevent bleeding. Put the whole beetroot into a well-buttered ovenproof dish and bake until tender.

When they are cooked, remove from the oven and peel. Quarter or slice the beetroot, return to the casserole and add the squeeze of lemon juice and salt and pepper to taste. Heat through before serving.

Rillettes De Porc *Potted Pork*

TOURAINE

The *charcuteries* and market stalls of the Touraine are full of stoneware pots of all sizes, sometimes covered with a pretty piece of gingham, containing rillettes de porc, for the district prides itself on making this preserve better than any other area of France. In spite of modern methods of refrigeration, this old farmhouse method of rendering down and preserving in fat is still used to make tasty *confits* of all kinds. Rillettes de porc are easy to make, keep well in the refrigerator for several weeks, and may be eaten cold as an hors d'oeuvre with mustard, or warmed, with mashed potatoes.

Preparation time: 30 minutes
Cooking time: 6 hours
To serve: 4 to 8

1 kg/2 lb belly of pork, skinned, boned and cut into 2.5 cm/1 inch cubes
1 teaspoon salt
½ teaspoon coarsely ground black pepper
1 bouquet garni (bay leaf and thyme and rosemary sprigs)
good pinch of ground allspice
¼ teaspoon grated nutmeg
¼ teaspoon ground cinnamon
¼ teaspoon ground cloves
50 g/2 oz lard (optional)

Put all the ingredients, except the lard, into a very heavy pan, wide enough, if possible, to allow all the meat to touch the bottom of the pan. Add just enough water to stop the meat from catching, cover the pan and melt over a very, very low heat for about 6 hours. Stir from time to time and add a little more water if necessary. The meat should become quite soft, but not totally disintegrated, and it must not be allowed to brown.

Strain off the liquid into a bowl and chill it in order to let the fat set. Put the meat into a large bowl. Remove the bouquet garni. Pound the meat with a wooden spoon or mallet, then pull it into threads with two forks. The mixture should become light and thready. You can process the meat briefly in small batches in a blender, but do not use a food processor.

Taste for seasoning; if underseasoned, return the meat to the cooking pot and add more seasoning to taste. Heat through to distribute the seasoning evenly.

Pot the meat mixture in prepared sterilized pots, preferably stoneware; glass preserving jars will also do. Gently warm the fat until just runny, then pour enough of it over the top of the pots to make a 1 cm/½ inch layer. Be careful not to include any of the meat juice that will have settled at the bottom of the bowl. If there is not enough fat, you may have to use some lard. Refrigerate overnight.

The next day, cover the pots with cling film and foil, or gingham, and tie on securely. If you are eating the rillettes cold, do not serve straight from the refrigerator, but allow at least 1 hour at room temperature before serving.

Salade De Pommes De Terre Parisienne *Potato Salad*

ILE DE FRANCE

This delicate potato salad must be made with waxy new potatoes that will keep their shape. It is excellent served plain, and even more delicious when some champignons de Paris, the slightly brown-tinged button mushrooms, are folded in gently just before serving.

Preparation time: 15 minutes
Cooking time: 15 to 20 minutes
To serve: 6

1 kg/2 lb new potatoes
300 ml/½ pint white wine
1 tablespoon wine vinegar
3 tablespoons corn or nut oil
salt
freshly ground black pepper
225 g/8 oz button mushrooms, thinly sliced and sprinkled with lemon juice (optional)
½ tablespoon finely chopped fresh parsley, chives or tarragon

Cook the potatoes in their skins in boiling water until they are just tender. Drain and peel them carefully. Slice fairly thinly into a bowl containing the wine. Turn once gently and leave to cool.

When the potatoes are cold, sprinkle on the vinegar, oil and salt and pepper to taste and turn very gently, being careful not to break the potatoes. Gently fold in the mushrooms, if used.

Sprinkle with the herbs just before serving.

Les Asperges *Asparagus*

ILE DE FRANCE

Asparagus is grown in many parts of France, but some of the best still comes from Argenteuil, on the outskirts of Paris. It is not quite as fat and white nor as highly prized as the asparagus of Cavaillon, but has a slightly green tinge and excellent flavour. There are many different ways of serving asparagus – cold, with a vinaigrette (see page 110) or mayonnaise – or hot, simply with melted butter, or, more elaborately, with a beurre blanc (see page 112), a sauce hollandaise (see page 113) or a sauce mousseline (see page 110). But the first consideration is to cook it well.

Preparation time: 10 minutes
Cooking time: 12 to 20 minutes
To serve: 2 to 3

0.5 kg/1 lb asparagus
salt

Take each asparagus spear individually, and hold it tip downwards. Using a small sharp kitchen knife, cut off any solidly wooden part at the bottom, then pare or shave off the tough outer skin, from the bottom upwards, for as far as necessary.

Tie the spears into convenient bundles, tying them twice, near the top and near the bottom. If you do not have a special asparagus pan, use a saucepan large enough to hold the bundles lying flat and lower them into boiling salted water. Bring back to the boil and boil steadily until the bottom ends of the asparagus are tender when tested with the sharp point of a knife. Lift out the bundles and drain.

Les asperges, salade de champignons à la crème (page 37) and salade de pommes de terre Parisienne

Mustard Pommery

Les Oeufs A L'Auvergnate *Eggs Baked with Cheese and Cream*

AUVERGNE

This delicate dish is made in Auvergne with the local Cantal cheese, a hard pressed cheese made from cow's milk. A Gruyère would be the nearest alternative. Serve one egg per person as an appetizer, two for a light main course.

Preparation time: 15 minutes
Cooking time: 10 minutes
Oven temperature: 180°C, 350°F, Gas Mark 4
To serve: 4 to 8

8 eggs, separated
salt
freshly ground black pepper
15 g/½ oz butter
4 tablespoons crème fraîche (see page 118) or double cream
75 g/3 oz Cantal or Gruyère cheese, coarsely grated

Season the egg whites with salt and pepper and beat them until stiff and dry.

Butter a large ring mould generously and spoon in the egg whites evenly, smoothing off the top. Make eight indentations with the back of a soup spoon at regular intervals and drop one egg yolk into each. Mask each yolk with the cream and sprinkle all over with the grated cheese.

Cook in the oven until just set and serve immediately.

Cèpes Au Gratin *Mushrooms Baked in Cream Sauce*

DAUPHINE

This area has a wealth of mushrooms – cèpes, morilles and chanterelles. Even using cultivated mushrooms, this simple dish makes a delicious appetizer.

Preparation time: 20 minutes
Cooking time: 20 minutes
To serve: 4

65 g/2½ oz butter
1 large onion, finely chopped
1 garlic clove, finely chopped
0.75 kg/1½ lb mushrooms, thinly sliced
salt
freshly ground black pepper
300 ml/½ pint crème fraiche (see page 118)
1 tablespoon fine dry white breadcrumbs
1 tablespoon finely grated cheese

Melt 50 g/2 oz of the butter in a heavy saucepan, add the onion and garlic and fry gently until softened. Add the mushrooms, cover and cook until they soften. Season to taste with salt and pepper.

Bring the crème fraiche to the boil in another saucepan. Add the juice drained off the mushroom mixture, stir well and boil gently until the cream thickens. Fold in the mushrooms.

Divide the mixture between buttered cocotte dishes, sprinkle with the breadcrumbs and cheese and dot with the remaining butter. Brown quickly under a hot grill and serve.

Flamiche Aux Poireaux *Leek Tart*

PICARDY

This creamy leek tart appears in different guises in various parts of Northern France, sometimes with diced cooked ham added to the filling, sometimes with a pastry lid, so that it becomes more of a pie than a tart. This is the 'pure' version as it is made in Picardy.

Preparation time: 30 minutes
Cooking time: 50 minutes
Oven temperature: 200°C, 400°F, Gas Mark 6
To serve: 6

½ quantity pâte brisée (see page 114)
100 g/4 oz butter
1.5 kg/3 lb leeks, white parts only, sliced (0.75 kg/1½ lb prepared weight)
2 tablespoons flour
300 ml/½ pint milk
pinch of grated nutmeg
salt
freshly ground black pepper
2 eggs
150 ml/¼ pint double cream
100 g/4 oz cheese, grated

Roll out the dough and use to line a 25 cm/10 inch flan tin. Prick the dough and bake blind for 10 minutes.

Melt half the butter in a heavy saucepan, add the leeks, cover and sweat very gently, without allowing to colour, for 10 minutes. Add just enough water to stop the leeks from burning and cook until tender.

In another saucepan melt 25 g/1 oz of the butter, stir in the flour and cook for 3 minutes without allowing to brown. Gradually stir in the milk and the cooking liquid from the leeks until smooth. Bring briefly to the boil, add the nutmeg and salt and pepper to taste and simmer the sauce for a few minutes, stirring well.

Spread the leeks out evenly in the pastry case.

Beat the eggs with the cream and add to the white sauce, together with half the grated cheese. Pour over the leeks. Sprinkle with the remaining cheese and dot with the remaining butter. Bake for a further 25 to 30 minutes or until the top is slightly risen and golden brown. Serve very hot.

Salade Chaude A La Flamande *Salad with Hot Dressing*

FLANDERS

This creamy salad dressing gives rather more body than usual to lettuce.

Preparation time: 10 minutes
Cooking time: 3 to 4 minutes
To serve: 4 to 6

2 good lettuces, leaves separated
4 eggs
2 tablespoons wine vinegar
salt
freshly ground black pepper
25 g/1 oz butter

Arrange the lettuce leaves in a salad bowl.

Break the eggs into a bowl, add the vinegar and salt and pepper to taste and beat together with a fork.

Melt the butter in a heavy saucepan, add the egg mixture and stir over a gentle heat until the eggs just begin to thicken. Pour quickly over the lettuce, turn it well and serve.

Feuilletés de Roquefort and pâte feuilletée (page 115)

Salade De Pissenlits Au Lard *Dandelion Salad with Bacon*

FLANDERS

Use young dandelion leaves, or, if your lawn does not grow enough of them, use one of the rather bitter salad greens such as curly endive, for this traditional country salad.

Preparation time: 10 minutes
Cooking time: 5 minutes
To serve: 4

1 curly endive or enough dandelion leaves
100 g/4 oz streaky bacon, finely diced
2 tablespoons wine vinegar
salt
freshly ground black pepper

Put the endive or dandelion leaves in a salad bowl.

Quickly fry the bacon dice in a frying pan until their fat has run and they are just beginning to crisp. Pour the contents of the frying pan, fat and all, over the salad. Add the vinegar to the pan, let it bubble up and pour over the salad also. Add salt and pepper to taste and turn well. Serve quickly.

Feuilletés De Roquefort *Roquefort Puffs*

LANGUEDOC

Made with the wonderful sheep's milk cheese that has to be matured in the particular caves of Roquefort in order to earn its name, these are delicious appetizers, or *bonnes bouchés* to accompany an aperitif.

Preparation time: 15 minutes (plus pastry)
Cooking time: 15 to 20 minutes
Oven temperature: 220°C, 425°F, Gas Mark 7
To serve: 6

⅔ quantity pâte feuilletée (see page 115) or puff pastry
225 g/8 oz Roquefort cheese
1 tablespoon brandy
2 tablespoons double cream
50 g/2 oz walnuts, finely chopped (optional)
1 small egg
1 tablespoon water

Roll out the dough 3 mm/⅛ inch thick. Cut into 7.5 cm/3 inch squares.

Crumble the cheese and blend it gently with the brandy, cream and walnuts, if used. There is no need to form a smooth paste.

Put a spoonful of the cheese mixture into the centre of each dough square. Moisten the edges and fold over into a triangle. Seal the edges well and crimp them together. Place the triangles on a baking sheet. Brush with the egg lightly beaten with the water and bake in the oven until puffed up and golden brown. Serve hot.

Salade Aux Noix *Salad with Walnuts*

PITOU

Walnut oil has a wonderful deep flavour, but, like the nuts themselves, must be used fresh or it becomes musty. Use the new season's oil, and always keep it in the refrigerator.

Preparation time: 15 minutes
To serve: 4 to 6

1 garlic clove, halved
1 lettuce
4 tablespoons walnut oil
1 slice of stale white bread, finely diced
50 g/2 oz walnuts, finely chopped
1 tablespoon wine vinegar
pinch of sugar
salt
freshly ground black pepper

Rub the inside of a salad bowl hard with the cut surface of the garlic clove. Tear the lettuce leaves into convenient pieces and put into the bowl.

Heat 1 tablespoon of the oil in a frying pan and quickly fry the diced bread, stirring well so that it browns on all sides. Scatter the bread croûtons over the lettuce leaves, together with the chopped walnuts.

Stir together the vinegar, sugar and salt and pepper to taste and slowly stir in the remaining walnut oil until the mixture is combined. Pour over the salad just before serving and toss well.

Les Artichauts A La Barigoule *Braised Artichokes*

PROVENCE

Use the small artichokes with pointed, purple-flushed leaves for this dish. They must be very young and fresh, so that they have not yet developed a hairy 'choke'. Serve as a hot hors d'oeuvre, allowing one or two artichokes per person.

Preparation time: 15 minutes
Cooking time: 15 to 20 minutes
To serve: 6

6 or 12 very young globe artichokes
150 ml/$\frac{1}{4}$ pint olive oil
150 ml/$\frac{1}{4}$ pint water
salt, preferably sea salt

Cut the stalks off the artichokes very close to the base, pull off the first layer of leaves and cut the remaining leaves down with kitchen scissors to within 2.5 cm/1 inch of the base, or to where the leaves begin to be fleshy.

Put the artichokes side by side into a heavy, wide-bottomed saucepan, add the oil and water and bring quickly to the boil. Boil, uncovered, until almost all the liquid has evaporated. The artichokes should have crisp brown outer leaves, and be quite tender inside, and it should be possible to eat them whole.

Place on individual plates, sprinkle with the remaining cooking liquid and a little salt and serve.

Caviar Provençal *Aubergine Dip*

PROVENCE

Nothing could be more satisfying than a bowl of this 'caviar', served with crusty French bread and a bottle of wine, for a light lunch, or to start a more substantial meal. The mixture can also be used for stuffing hard-boiled eggs, or served with raw vegetables (*crudités*), to make a more elaborate hors d'oeuvre.

Preparation time: about 45 minutes
Cooking time: 45 minutes to 1 hour
Oven temperature: 190°C, 375°F, Gas Mark 5
To serve: 6

1 kg/2 lb aubergines
3 garlic cloves, crushed
4 tablespoons olive oil
juice of $\frac{1}{2}$ lemon
salt
freshly ground black pepper
chopped fresh parsley or 1 anchovy fillet to garnish

Slice the aubergines in half lengthways and either grill very gently on both sides until very soft, or bake in the top of the oven. This may take up to 1 hour, and you must be careful not to let the skin burn. Scoop out the flesh and place in a blender or mortar, together with the garlic. Blend together, then slowly add the oil, drop by drop, as for making mayonnaise. Add the lemon juice and season to taste with salt and pepper.

Serve in a bowl, garnished with parsley or a rolled anchovy fillet.

Salade De Champignons A La Crème *Raw Mushroom Salad*

ORLEANNAIS

Creamy mushroom salad in thick brown bowls can be bought by weight in *charcuteries* and *alimentations* and sometimes even at market stalls. It should be made with the brown-tinged champignons de Paris or with field mushrooms, but cultivated button mushrooms will also do. Moutarde de Meaux, the lovely grainy mustard made in the town of Meaux, not far from Paris, should ideally be used. Serve alone or as part of a mixed hors d'oeuvre.

Preparation time: 10 minutes
To serve: 4

225 g/8 oz button mushrooms, trimmed
lemon juice
2 teaspoons Moutarde de Meaux or Dijon mustard
150 ml/$\frac{1}{4}$ pint crème fraîche (see page 118) or double cream
salt
freshly ground black pepper
1 tablespoon finely chopped fresh parsley

Sprinkle the mushrooms with a little lemon juice.

Stir the mustard into the cream and season it generously with salt and pepper. If you are using double cream, add some extra lemon juice.

Fold the mushrooms into the cream, pile into a dark glazed bowl and sprinkle with the parsley before serving.

Salade Bourguignonne *Salad with Chicken Livers*

BURGUNDY

Chicken livers are to Bresse what goose liver is to the Alsace and the Perigord, and they are used in countless unexpected ways. This is a most unusual salad, which can be served on its own as a first course.

Preparation time: 10 minutes
Cooking time: 3 minutes
To serve: 4

50 g/2 oz butter
100 g/4 oz chicken livers, roughly chopped
1 teaspoon Dijon mustard
1 tablespoon wine vinegar
1 egg yolk
3 tablespoons oil
salt
freshly ground black pepper
1 lettuce

Melt the butter in a frying pan, add the chicken livers and fry for 3 minutes – they should be just pink and set. Remove from the heat and chop finely.

Put the mustard into a bowl and stir in the vinegar. Add the egg yolk and stir until smooth. Dribble in the oil, stirring all the time to combine. Season to taste with salt and pepper and stir in the chicken livers.

Arrange the lettuce leaves in a salad bowl, pour over the chicken liver dressing and serve.

Terrine De Porc Pork Terrine

GASCOGNE

A robust coarse-textured country pâté, this is traditionally made when a pig has been killed on the farm. It makes an excellent mainstay for a summer lunch or buffet, served thickly sliced from an earthenware terrine.

Preparation time: 20 minutes (plus setting)
Cooking time: 1½ to 1¾ hours
Oven temperature: 220°C, 425°F, Gas Mark 7; reduced to 190°C, 375°F, Gas Mark 5
To serve: 8 to 12

1 kg/2 to 2¼ lb belly of pork, skinned and boned
225 g/8 oz pig's liver
1 onion, finely chopped
2 garlic cloves, finely chopped
2 fresh rosemary branches
1 egg
2 tablespoons brandy
salt
freshly ground black pepper
1 pig's trotter, split in half
2 bay leaves

Mince the pork coarsely with the liver. Mix in the onion and garlic and the finely chopped leaves of one of the rosemary branches.

Beat the egg with the brandy and season well with salt and pepper. Mix into the meat. Fry a small pat of the mixture to taste for seasoning. Press the mixture evenly into a 1 litre/2 pint terrine.

Blanch the pig's trotter in boiling water for 2 minutes, then drain and press into the top of the terrine, together with the second branch of rosemary and the bay leaves. Place the terrine in a roasting pan, add cold water to the pan to come halfway up the terrine and place in the oven. Reduce the heat after 15 minutes, and continue to cook until the meat has shrunk away from the sides of the dish and the cooking juices are clear.

Remove the trotter, smooth over the top and rearrange the rosemary and bay leaves. Leave to cool slightly, then weight down the pâté and leave for at least 1 day before serving, to allow it to set firmly and for the flavour to mature.

Pâté De Foie De Volaille Poultry Liver Pâté

ALSACE

Strasbourg is the home of foie gras, the grossly enlarged liver of geese that have been force-fed, and from which an amazingly rich pâté is made, sometimes enriched further still by the truffles of the Perigord district. That is a dish best left to the professionals, but a rich smooth pâté made of chicken livers or of a mixture of chicken and duck, and even on occasion a goose liver, is a treat that is very easy for the housewife to make.

Preparation time: 10 minutes (plus setting)
Cooking time: 7 minutes
To serve: 10 to 12

225 g/8 oz butter
0.5 kg/1 lb poultry livers (see above)
2 tablespoons brandy
2 tablespoons Madeira
2 garlic cloves
¼ teaspoon dried mixed herbs
salt
freshly ground black pepper
1 bay leaf

Melt half the butter in a heavy frying pan, add the livers and cook them over a moderate heat for 5 minutes, stirring so that they cook evenly. The livers should be brown on the outside, and pink, but set, in the centre.

Pour the contents of the frying pan into a blender or food processor. Pour the brandy and Madeira into the pan and bring quickly to the boil, stirring well to incorporate any sediment left on the bottom of the pan. Allow to bubble for 1 minute, then add to the livers. Add the garlic and dried herbs and blend until smooth. Blend in the remaining butter and salt and pepper to taste.

Pour into one or several earthenware terrines, place a bay leaf on top and refrigerate overnight before serving.

If the pâté is to be kept for several days before serving, pour enough cooled, melted butter over the top to form a complete seal. The pâté will then keep for at least a week in the refrigerator.

Foie De Volaille Aux Raisins *Poultry Livers with Grapes*

GUYENNE

This southwest corner of France is famous above all for its fatted geese and their foie gras, sometimes weighing as much as 1 kg/2.2 lb each. These are not only made into the world-renowned truffled pâté but are also sometimes served quite simply fried in butter. So are the livers of ducks and turkeys which are also raised a great deal here. Combined with the local chasselas grapes, they make a simple but rich and delicious first course or light dish. Use the liver of whichever bird you are cooking, and supplement with chicken livers if necessary.

Preparation time: 10 minutes
Cooking time: 10 minutes
To serve: 4 to 6

0.5 kg/1 lb poultry livers (see above)
175 g/6 oz butter
4 to 6 slices of white bread
salt
freshly ground black pepper
150 ml/$\frac{1}{4}$ pint white wine or dry vermouth
225 g/8 oz white grapes, peeled and pipped

Pick over the livers and cut the larger livers of geese, turkeys or ducks into thick slices. Leave chicken livers whole.

Melt 50 g/2 oz of the butter in a heavy frying pan and quickly brown the slices of bread on both sides. Set aside and keep warm on a heated serving plate.

Add the remaining butter to the clean frying pan and when it begins to foam put in the livers, spreading them out so that they can cook evenly. Cook for 3 minutes on each side, but no more – they should be brown on the outside and pink but set inside. Season generously with salt and pepper and divide between the pieces of fried bread. Keep hot.

Add the wine or vermouth to the pan, stir well to loosen any sediment and bring quickly to the boil. Boil for 1 minute to reduce. Add the grapes to the pan and allow to heat through, then pour over the livers. Serve hot.

Terrine de porc and foie de volaille aux raisins

Quiche Lorraine *Bacon and Egg Tart*

LORRAINE

This well-known speciality should be just creamily set and delicately flavoured with the smoked ham of the region. Failing this, smoked pork or bacon may also be used.

Preparation time: 15 minutes (plus pastry)
Cooking time: 45 to 50 minutes
Oven temperature: 190°C, 375°F, Gas Mark 5
To serve: 4 to 6

225 g/8 oz pâte brisée (see page 114)
100 g/4 oz smoked ham, pork or bacon, cubed
3 eggs
300 ml/½ pint crème fraîche (see page 118) or double cream
salt
freshly ground black pepper

Roll out the dough and use to line a 23 cm/9 inch flan tin, preferably one with a removable base. Prick the dough all over with a fork and bake blind for 10 minutes.

Meanwhile, fry the ham, pork or bacon lightly in a frying pan to let some of the fat run. Drain on paper towels.

Beat the eggs in a bowl together with the cream. Season to taste with salt and pepper. Scatter the pieces of ham, pork or bacon evenly over the bottom of the pastry case. Pour in the egg and cream mixture and return to the oven. Bake for a further 35 to 40 minutes or until the eggs have just set and the top of the filling is golden. Check the quiche from time to time and prick any bubbles that may form. Serve hot or cold.

Quiche Aux Oignons *Alsatian Onion Tart*

ALSACE

This creamy flan has a strong onion flavour.

Preparation time: 30 minutes (plus pastry)
Cooking time: 30 minutes
Oven temperature: 220°C, 425°F, Gas Mark 7
To serve: 6

225 g/8 oz pâte brisée (see page 114)
50 g/2 oz lard
0.5 kg/1 lb onions, thinly sliced
100 g/4 oz smoked pork or bacon, diced
salt
freshly ground black pepper
25 g/1 oz butter
25 g/1 oz flour
300 ml/½ pint milk
1 egg yolk
1 tablespoon crème fraîche (see page 118) or double cream
good pinch of grated nutmeg

Roll out the dough and use to line a 23 cm/9 inch flan tin, preferably one with a removable base. Prick the dough all over with a fork and bake blind for 10 minutes.

Melt the lard in a frying pan and add the onions. Cook them over a moderately high heat until they are just golden brown. If you are using bacon, fry it together with the onions and use a little less lard. Season to taste with salt and pepper. Remove from the heat.

Melt the butter in a saucepan, stir in the flour and cook over a gentle heat for 3 minutes without allowing to brown. Add the milk and stir until you have a smooth sauce. Bring to the boil, then lower the heat and simmer, stirring, until the sauce thickens.

Distribute the onions and the smoked pork or bacon evenly over the bottom of the pastry case. Mix the egg yolk with the cream and add to the sauce. Season to taste with salt and pepper and add the nutmeg. Pour the sauce evenly into the pastry case and return to the oven. Bake for a further 20 minutes or until the filling is set. Serve very hot.

Fish and Shellfish

Homard Grillé Grilled Lobster in Cream Sauce

BRITANNY

'Homard à l'Amoricaine', as the Bretons insist that it should really be called after the ancient name of the kingdom of Brittany, is one of the classic restaurant dishes that are perhaps more hallowed by reputation than by eating. This is a simplified version, which is nonetheless rich and wonderful for a special occasion. A similar dish is also made with crayfish that are caught off the Breton coast.

Preparation time: 30 minutes
Cooking time: 30 minutes
To serve: 2 to 3

1 lobster, cooked
225 g/8 oz tomatoes, skinned and roughly chopped
2 tablespoons finely chopped shallots
150 ml/$\frac{1}{4}$ pint white wine
300 ml/$\frac{1}{2}$ pint double cream
15 g/$\frac{1}{2}$ oz flour
15 g/$\frac{1}{2}$ oz butter
1 teaspoon Dijon mustard
salt
freshly ground black pepper
2 tablespoons brandy
1 tablespoon finely grated Parmesan, Gruyère or Cheddar cheese

Extract the lobster meat from the shell, discarding the grey sac in the head and the intestinal canal that runs through the body and tail. Arrange the meat in a gratin dish and keep warm.

Put the tomatoes, shallots and white wine in a saucepan, bring to the boil and simmer until reduced to a soft purée.

Bring the cream to the boil in another saucepan and simmer until it begins to thicken.

Make a beurre manié by working the flour into the butter. Add this to the cream and stir until smooth. Pass the tomato mixture through a fine sieve and add the purée to the cream. Add the mustard and salt and pepper to taste. Bring quickly to almost boiling point.

Warm the brandy, set alight and pour over the lobster. Pour on the sauce, which should completely cover the lobster, smooth the top and sprinkle with the cheese. Heat through and brown quickly under a hot grill before serving.

Moules A La Marinière Mussels Cooked in White Wine

BRITTANY

The most classic of all the mussel dishes, this is usually served from a big tureen. Everyone helps themselves into deep soup plates, and a few extra plates are left on the table for the discarded mussel shells. Experienced mussel eaters use an empty double shell in a pincer action to eat each mussel, and an empty single shell to scoop up the delicious liquid. All else that is needed is chunks of French bread for mopping up, and a few finger bowls.

Preparation time: 20 minutes (plus cleaning mussels)
Cooking time: 6 minutes
To serve: 6 to 8

1 bottle of white wine
2 onions, finely chopped
1 bouquet garni
3 litres/5 pints mussels, cleaned
2 tablespoons finely chopped fresh parsley

Put the wine in a very large saucepan together with the onions and the bouquet garni and bring to the boil. Boil rapidly for about 3 minutes in order to evaporate the liquid a little.

Add the mussels, cover the pan and cook over a high heat until the mussels open. Shake the pan occasionally so that the mussels will change position and cook evenly. If the pan is too heavy to shake effectively, use a slotted spoon to move the mussels around.

Discard any mussels that remain closed after 6 minutes and pour the remainder into the heated tureen. Sprinkle with the parsley and serve very hot.

Crabe Gratinée A La Bretonne *Crab in Cream Sauce*

BRITTANY

A very rich and filling but quite inexpensive dish, this can be served as an appetizer or main course. Spider crabs may also be used.

Preparation time: 30 minutes
Cooking time: 20 minutes
To serve: 4 to 6

2 large crabs, cooked
100 g/4 oz butter
50 g/2 oz flour
150 ml/¼ pint white wine
600 ml/1 pint milk
salt and freshly ground black pepper
2 tablespoons crème fraîche (see page 118) or double cream
1 egg yolk
salt
freshly ground black pepper
1 tablespoon fine dry white breadcrumbs

Extract all the meat from the crabs and set aside. Scrub the body shells and reserve.

Melt 75 g/3 oz of the butter in a large saucepan. Stir in the flour and cook, without allowing to brown, for 3 minutes. Add the wine and stir to a smooth paste. Slowly stir in the milk until smooth and simmer for 5 minutes.

Mix the crème fraîche with the egg yolk and add to the pan with salt and pepper to taste. Stir in the crab meat. Spoon the mixture into the crab shells; pour any that is left over into a shallow gratin dish. Sprinkle with the breadcrumbs, dot with the remaining butter and brown quickly under a hot grill.

Crabe gratinée a la Bretonne, homard grillé and moules à la marinière

Mouclade *Mussels in Cream Sauce*

BRITTANY

This is a richer and more elegant dish than Moules à la Marinière, suitable for formal occasions. In a restaurant the mussels would probably be served each in their half shell, but for cooking at home it is simpler to serve them in a gratin dish without the shells.

Preparation time: 20 minutes (plus cleaning mussels)
Cooking time: 15 minutes
To serve: 6 as a main dish, or 10 as an appetizer

450 ml/¾ pint white wine
1 onion, finely chopped
1 garlic clove, finely chopped
1 bouquet garni (bay leaf and parsley and fennel sprigs)
½ teaspoon curry powder
3 litres/5 pints mussels, cleaned
65 g/2½ oz butter
25 g/1 oz flour
150 ml/¼ pint crème fraîche (see page 118)
2 egg yolks
good squeeze lemon juice
salt
freshly ground black pepper
1 tablespoon finely chopped fresh parsley

Put the wine in a wide saucepan together with the onion, garlic, bouquet garni and curry powder, and bring to the boil. Add the mussels, cover the pan and cook over a high heat until the mussels open. Shake the pan occasionally so that the mussels will change position and cook evenly. If the pan is too heavy to shake effectively, use a slotted spoon to move the mussels around.

Remove the mussels with a slotted spoon as they open and discard any that remain closed after 6 minutes. Discard the shells and arrange the mussels in a heated gratin dish. Keep warm.

Boil the cooking liquid rapidly for a few minutes to reduce. Strain and reserve 450 ml/¾ pint. In a clean pan melt 50 g/2 oz of the butter, add the flour and cook gently, without allowing to brown, for 3 minutes. Slowly stir in the reserved cooking liquid until smooth, then bring to the boil and simmer for 1 to 2 minutes or until the sauce thickens.

Mix the crème fraîche with the egg yolks and lemon juice. Stir in a little of the hot sauce, then add to the remaining sauce in the pan. Stir in salt and pepper to taste. Add the remaining butter, cut into very small pieces, to give the sauce a glaze; pour it over the mussels in the dish and sprinkle with the parsley before serving.

Truites A La Bretonne *Fried Trout with Potatoes and Capers*

BRITTANY

An 'all in one' dish, this tastes every bit as good as it looks.

Preparation time: 15 minutes
Cooking time: 25 minutes
To serve: 4

4 trout, cleaned
2 tablespoons flour
salt
freshly ground black pepper
100 g/4 oz butter
2 tablespoons oil
0.5 kg/1 lb potatoes, peeled and diced
100 g/4 oz cooked prawns or shrimps, peeled
2 tablespoons roughly chopped capers
1 tablespoon finely chopped fresh parsley

Dry the trout on paper towels, then coat them in the well-seasoned flour. Brush excess flour off so that they have just a thin even covering.

Melt half the butter with 1 tablespoon of the oil in a heavy frying pan. Add the potatoes and cook over a moderate heat until tender and beginning to brown, turning from time to time.

Meanwhile, melt the remaining butter with the remaining oil in another large heavy frying pan. When sizzling hot, put in the trout. Cook for 8 to 10 minutes on each side – they should be cooked and golden brown, with a crisp skin.

Add the prawns or shrimps and the capers to the potatoes. Heat through, then add salt and pepper to taste.

Arrange the trout on a heated serving dish, scatter the potato, prawn and caper mixture over and around the trout and sprinkle with the parsley. Serve very hot.

Filets De Sole Deauville *Fillets of Sole with Onion Sauce*

NORMANDY

Onion and sole blend remarkably well in this dish, which combines so many of Normandy's favourite products.

Preparation time: 15 minutes
Cooking time: 30 minutes
To serve: 4

3 to 4 sole, filleted and bones reserved
1 small onion, quartered
150 ml/$\frac{1}{4}$ pint cider
1 lemon slice
1 bay leaf
1 parsley sprig
65 g/2$\frac{1}{2}$ oz butter
225 g/8 oz onions, finely chopped
150ml/$\frac{1}{4}$ pint crème fraîche (see page 118)
pinch of grated nutmeg
$\frac{1}{2}$ teaspoon French mustard
squeeze of lemon juice
salt
freshly ground black pepper
2 tablespoons fine dry white breadcrumbs

Put the fish bones in a large saucepan, add the quartered onion, cider, lemon slice, bay leaf and parsley and cover with cold water. Bring to the boil and boil rapidly for 10 minutes. Strain the stock.

Melt 50 g/2 oz of the butter in a heavy saucepan, add the chopped onions and cook very gently until they are quite soft and almost puréed, but barely coloured.

Meanwhile poach the fish fillets in the fish stock for 5 minutes. Lift them out gently and place in a buttered gratin dish. Keep warm. Reserve the stock.

Add 4 tablespoons of the fish stock to the onions, then stir in the crème fraîche, nutmeg, mustard, lemon juice and salt and pepper to taste. Pour the sauce over the sole, sprinkle on the breadcrumbs and dot with the remaining butter. Brown quickly under a hot grill before serving.

Coquilles St Jacques A La Dieppoise

Scallops with Shrimps and Mussels
NORMANDY

These are most attractive when served in the deeper top shells of the scallops. If frozen scallops have to be used, the dish may be cooked in small cocotte dishes. One per person makes a delicious appetizer, two an ample main dish.

Preparation time: 15 minutes (plus cleaning mussels)
Cooking time: 30 minutes
To serve: 4 or 8 (see above)

300 ml/½ pint mussels, cleaned
150 ml/¼ pint white wine or cider
150 ml/¼ pint water
8 scallops, detached from their shells and cleaned
100 g/4 oz button mushrooms, quartered
1 onion, finely chopped
100 g/4 oz cooked shrimps or prawns, peeled
25 g/1 oz flour
50 g/2 oz butter
4 tablespoons crème fraîche (see page 118) or double cream
salt
freshly ground black pepper
2 tablespoons fine dry white breadcrumbs

Put the mussels in a large saucepan with half the wine or cider and half the water. Cover the pan and cook over a high heat until the mussels open. Remove the mussels with a slotted spoon as soon as they have opened, take the meat from the shells and set aside. Discard any mussels that remain closed. Strain the cooking liquid and reserve.

Put the scallops (white and coral), mushrooms and onion in another saucepan, add the remaining wine or cider and water and poach for 6 to 8 minutes, until the scallops are opaque and tender. Remove from the heat. Take out the scallops with a slotted spoon and place one in each well-washed scallop shell. Surround with the poached mushrooms, shrimps or prawns and mussels.

Add the mussel liquid to the liquid left in the pan and boil briskly for 2 minutes to reduce. Strain and return to the pan.

Make a beurre manié by working the flour into half the butter. Add to the pan and simmer, stirring, for 2 minutes. Stir in the crème fraîche and salt and pepper to taste. Pour the sauce gently over the scallops in the shells, sprinkle with the breadcrumbs and dot with the remaining butter. Heat through and brown under a hot grill.

Harengs A La Dieppoise

NORMANDY

Made in this harbour town, with herrings fresh from the sea, this is a delicious hors d'oeuvre.

Preparation time: 10 minutes (plus cooling)
Cooking time: 15 to 20 minutes
To serve: 6

300 ml/½ pint white wine or cider
150 ml/¼ pint wine vinegar
150 ml/¼ pint water
1 carrot, thinly sliced
2 onions, cut into rings
1 bouquet garni
12 peppercorns, lightly crushed
6 fresh herrings, cleaned
1 lemon, sliced

Put the wine or cider in a wide saucepan with the vinegar, water, carrot, 1 onion, the bouquet garni and peppercorns. Bring to the boil and boil briskly for 5 minutes.

Lower the heat and put the herrings into the pan. Poach very gently for 10 to 12 minutes or until cooked. The herrings must not be allowed to disintegrate. Remove from the heat.

Leave the herrings to cool in the marinade, preferably overnight. Lift out with a fish slice and arrange on a shallow serving dish. Strain over the marinade. Garnish with the second onion and the lemon slices.

Coquilles gratinées St Michel, harengs à la Dieppoise and coquilles St Jacques à la Dieppoise

Coquilles Gratinées St Michel

Scallops with Cheese and Cream

NORMANDY

A very simple way of cooking scallops, this is nonetheless very rich. Serve in the deep top scallop shell if possible, as in the previous recipe. One per person makes a delicious first course, two a good main dish.

Preparation time: 15 minutes
Cooking time: 30 minutes
To serve: 4 or 8 (see above)

8 scallops, detached from their shells and cleaned
1 onion, finely chopped
150 ml/$\frac{1}{4}$ pint white wine or cider
150 ml/$\frac{1}{4}$ pint water
25 g/1 oz flour
65 g/$2\frac{1}{2}$ oz butter
2 tablespoons finely grated Gruyère, Parmesan or Cheddar cheese
4 tablespoons crème fraîche (see page 118) or double cream
salt
freshly ground black pepper
2 tablespoons fine dry white breadcrumbs

Put the scallops (white and coral) into a saucepan with the onion, wine or cider and water and poach for 6 to 8 minutes or until the scallops are opaque and tender. Remove the scallops from the pan with a slotted spoon, slice thickly and set aside.

Boil the cooking liquid briskly for 2 minutes to reduce, then strain and return to the pan. Make a beurre manié by working the flour into 50 g/2 oz of the butter. Add to the pan and simmer, stirring, for 2 minutes. Stir in half the cheese, the crème fraîche and salt and pepper to taste.

Return the scallops to the sauce and heat through, then pour into the scallop shells. Sprinkle with the breadcrumbs mixed with the remaining cheese, dot with the remaining butter and brown quickly under a hot grill.

Sole Dieppoise *Fillets of Sole with Mussels*

NORMANDY

Ancestor of the restaurant favourite, 'sole normande', which was in fact invented by a Parisian restaurateur (perhaps even the great Carême?), this is a simpler country version.

Preparation time: 15 minutes (plus cleaning mussels)
Cooking time: 30 minutes
Oven temperature: 180°C, 350°F, Gas Mark 4
To serve: 4

4 sole, cleaned and skinned
salt
freshly ground black pepper
450 ml/¾ pint white wine or cider
1 litre/1¾ pints mussels, cleaned
1 onion, finely chopped
2 parsley sprigs
40 g/1½ oz butter
25 g/1 oz flour
600 ml/1 pint cooked shrimps, peeled (optional)
squeeze of lemon juice

Season the sole well with salt and pepper on both sides and lay in a shallow, enamelled or porcelain, ovenproof dish. Pour on half the white wine or cider, cover with greaseproof or wax paper and foil and cook in the oven for 10 to 15 minutes, according to size.

Meanwhile put the mussels in a large saucepan with the remaining wine or cider, half the chopped onion and the parsley. Cover the pan and cook over a high heat until the mussels open. Remove the mussels with a slotted spoon as soon as they open, take the meat from the shells and keep warm. Discard any mussels that remain closed. Strain the cooking liquid and reserve.

In another saucepan, melt 25 g/1 oz of the butter, add the remaining onion and cook over a gentle heat until soft. Sprinkle on the flour and cook, stirring and not allowing to brown, for 3 minutes. Slowly add the strained mussel cooking liquid.

When the sole is cooked, remove it from the oven and pour off the liquid into another saucepan. Boil briskly until reduced almost to a glaze. Add to the sauce.

Arrange the mussels and shrimps, if used, round the sole in the ovenproof dish. Add the lemon juice to the sauce and adjust the seasoning. Add the remaining butter, cut into small pieces, to give the sauce a glaze. Pour over the fish, return to the oven for a few minutes to reheat and serve.

Truite Saumonée A L'Oseille *Salmon Trout with Sorrel Sauce*

NIVERNAIS

Salmon trout are often served in the Loire area, sometimes, as here, with a green purée of sorrel – a feast for the eyes as well as the palate. Salmon steaks may be cooked in the same way, with the steaks laid on a bed of sorrel purée.

Preparation time: 30 minutes
Cooking time: about 20 minutes
Oven temperature: 180°C, 350°F, Gas Mark 4
To serve: 4 to 6

50 g/2 oz butter
1 tablespoon finely chopped shallots
0.5 kg/1 lb sorrel leaves, stripped off the thicker stalks
dash of dry vermouth
salt
freshly ground black pepper
pinch of grated nutmeg
150 ml/¼ pint crème fraîche (see page 118)
1 salmon trout, cleaned and gutted
150 ml/¼ pint dry white wine

Melt the butter in a heavy saucepan, add the shallots and fry until softened. Add the sorrel leaves and the vermouth, cover the pan and cook for a few minutes until the sorrel has wilted and is almost puréed. Add salt and pepper to taste and the nutmeg and stir in half the cream.

Stuff the trout with this mixture, and lay it in a buttered shallow ovenproof dish. Pour on the wine, cover with a sheet of buttered paper and then foil and cook in the oven until done. The time taken will vary with the size of the fish; you should lift the foil and test after 20 minutes, as the fish should not be allowed to overcook.

When ready, pour off the cooking juice into a small saucepan, add the remaining cream and bring quickly to the boil. Boil for 1 to 2 minutes to reduce. Adjust the seasoning, then pour gently around the fish and serve.

Matelote De Maqueraux *Mackerel Stewed in Wine*

ARTOIS

A sturdy fisherman's stew, this is made here with the mackerel that are caught in great abundance in the short stretch of water that divides England from France around Calais and Boulogne. In other parts of France it may be made with eel – not so dissimilar from mackerel in their rich meatiness. Further south, in Burgundy, a similar dish will be made using red wine.

Preparation time: 20 minutes
Cooking time: 30 minutes
To serve: 6

75 g/3 oz butter
1 large onion, sliced
1 large carrot, sliced
1 garlic clove, finely chopped
3 large mackerel, gutted and cut into 5 cm/2 inch slices
300 ml/½ pint dry white wine
1 bouquet garni (bay leaf, parsley and fennel)
salt
freshly ground black pepper
225 g/8 oz button mushrooms

Melt 50 g/2 oz of the butter in a heavy saucepan, add the vegetables and sweat gently until soft. Do not allow them to brown.

Lay the pieces of mackerel on top of the bed of vegetables, add the wine, bouquet garni and salt and pepper to taste and bring to the boil. Cover and simmer for 15 to 20 minutes or until the fish is just done, but has not begun to disintegrate.

While the fish is cooking, melt the remaining butter in a frying pan, add the mushrooms and fry quickly over a high heat.

Lift the fish out carefully with a slotted spoon and place in a heated tureen. Add some of the pieces of carrot and the onion slices. Scatter the mushrooms over the fish. Bring the remaining cooking liquid to the boil and boil fiercely for 2 minutes to reduce. Pour it over the fish and serve.

Truite Au Riesling *Trout Cooked in Riesling*

ALSACE

A perfect marriage of the fresh little trout from the mountain streams and the sparklingly crisp dry local wine, this dish is a speciality of the mountainous Vosges.

Preparation time: 15 minutes
Cooking time: 25 minutes
Oven temperature: 200°C, 400°F, Gas Mark 6
To serve: 4

4 trout, cleaned
salt
freshly ground black pepper
65 g/2½ oz butter
2 tablespoons finely chopped shallots
250 ml/scant ½ pint Riesling or dry white wine
100 g/4 oz mushrooms, thinly sliced
150 ml/¼ pint crème fraîche (see page 118) or double cream

Garnish
½ tablespoon finely chopped fresh parsley
4 lemon slices

Wipe the trout inside and out and season lightly with salt and pepper. Melt 25 g/1 oz of the butter in a small saucepan, add the shallots and fry until softened. Spread the shallots on the bottom of a shallow ovenproof dish, wide enough to hold the trout lying side by side. Lay the trout on top. Bring the wine quickly to the boil in the saucepan and pour over the trout in the dish. Cover with buttered paper and then with foil, place in the oven and cook for 10 to 15 minutes, according to the size of the trout.

Soften the mushrooms in 25 g/1 oz of the butter and season lightly with salt and pepper.

When the fish is cooked, remove it from the oven and carefully pour off the cooking liquor. Strain this into a clean saucepan, bring to the boil and boil rapidly, uncovered, until it has reduced by about half.

Meanwhile take the skin very carefully off the trout, being careful not to let them break up. If they seem too delicate to turn over, take the skin off the top only.

When the cooking liquor has begun to thicken, pour in the juice from the mushrooms and stir in the cream. Adjust the seasoning and add the mushrooms and the remaining butter, cut into small pieces, to give the sauce a glaze. Pour the sauce carefully over the trout and garnish each fish with a parsley-sprinkled slice of lemon. Serve hot.

Cabillaud A La Flamande Cod à la Flamande

FLANDERS

Cod is a fish which is often dried, salted and served in a stew in France. The fresh version is found mostly on the north-western sea coast where this delicious treatment originates.

Preparation time: 15 minutes
Cooking time: 15 minutes
Oven temperature: 180°C, 350°F, Gas Mark 4
To serve: 4

1 kg/2 lb fresh cod fillet, cut into 4 equal pieces
salt
freshly ground black pepper
50 g/2 oz butter
1 tablespoon chopped shallots
2 tablespoons chopped fresh parsley
150 ml/¼ pint dry white wine
4 slices of lemon

Season the fresh cod pieces with salt and freshly ground black pepper. Place the fillets side by side in a flameproof casserole, which has been rubbed generously with some of the butter, and sprinkled with the shallots and a tablespoon of the fresh parsley. Pour the dry white wine over the fish. On each piece place a slice of lemon. Bring to the boil on top of the stove, then cover and place in the oven for about 12 minutes to finish cooking.

Remove the cod from the oven, and drain, reserving the pan juices. Place the fish on a heated serving plate. Bring the juices to the boil on top of the cooker, reduce by half, and add the remaining butter. Pour over the fish and sprinkle with the chopped fresh parsley.

Poisson Grillé Au Fenouil *Grilled Fish with Fennel*

PROVENCE

Any very fresh, medium-sized fish, such as bass, bream or mullet, is excellent prepared in this way, especially if cooked out of doors over charcoal, to which a few branches of fennel have been added. But even cooked indoors, under the grill, it is delicious, and the combination of the aniseed flavour of the fennel with the slightly charred skin and moist flesh of fresh fish is quite irresistible.

Preparation time: 10 minutes (plus making butter)
Cooking time: 15 to 25 minutes
To serve: 6

3 kg/6½ lb fish (see above), allowing 1 small or ½ larger fish per person, cleaned and scaled
bunch of fresh fennel
salt
freshly ground black pepper
lemon juice
2 tablespoons olive oil
Montpelier butter (see page 111) to garnish

Cut deep diagonal slashes in the side of the fish, and insert a sprig of fennel in each. Place a sprig of fennel in the cavity of each fish also, together with a good sprinkling of salt and pepper. Rub the outside of each fish with salt and pepper and place them on the grid of the barbecue or wire rack of the grill pan. If using a grill pan, line it with foil to catch the juices.

Dribble some lemon juice and olive oil over each fish, put another sprig of fennel on top of each one and place under the very hot grill or over the hot charcoal embers.

When one side of the fish is done, and its skin is lightly charred, turn over carefully. Sprinkle the other side with lemon juice and oil, place another branch of fennel on top and cook until this side is done also. Pour the cooking juices over the fish when serving, with Montpelier butter.

Beurre de Montpellier (page 111), gigot de mer with ratatouille, and poisson grillé au fenouil

Gigot De Mer *Baked Fish*

PROVENCE

A whole sea bass, or a large piece of monkfish, is often spiked with garlic and baked in the oven, just like a leg of lamb – hence the name.
It may be served with a salad, but is more often served in Provence with a ratatouille, as below.

Preparation time: 15 minutes (plus making ratatouille)
Cooking time: 30 to 40 minutes
Oven temperature: 190°C, 375°F, Gas Mark 5
To serve: 6

2 to 2.5 kg/4½ to 5½ lb whole fish or thick slice, cleaned and scaled
2 garlic cloves, cut into slivers
1 tablespoon olive oil
2 onions, thinly sliced
2 bay leaves
salt
freshly ground black pepper
1 fresh thyme sprig
2 fresh parsley sprigs
1 lemon, thinly sliced
150 ml/¼ pint dry white wine or dry vermouth
ratatouille (see page 105)

Cut diagonal slits all over the surface of the fish, and insert a sliver of garlic in each.

Line a baking dish with foil and oil the foil with about 1 teaspoon of the olive oil. Use half the sliced onion to make a bed for the fish, top with a bay leaf and lay the fish on top. Put salt, pepper, thyme and parsley inside the fish and cover with the remaining onion and bay leaf and half the lemon slices. Dribble on the remaining olive oil. Pour over the wine or vermouth and bake for 30 to 40 minutes, basting from time to time, until the fish is just cooked. Test by inserting a knife gently near the backbone – the fish should come away fairly easily and be only the palest pink.

Spread the ratatouille in a shallow ovenproof dish.

Remove the fish carefully from the baking dish onto a plate. Discard the bay leaves and lemon slices, then pour the remaining contents of the baking dish over the ratatouille.

Fillet the fish carefully and lay it, skin side up, on top of the ratatouille. Return to the oven briefly to heat through, and serve garnished with the remaining lemon slices.

Truite Au Jambon Bayonne *Trout with Bayonne Ham*

BEARN

Bayonne, in the southwest corner of France, is the coastal outpost of French Basque cuisine. It is famous for its fish, peppers and, especially, its ham. Like Italian Parma and German Westphalian hams, it is usually smoked and aged, then sliced very thinly and served raw as a first course. In this recipe, its delicate smokey flavour is a perfect foil to the buttery, flaky trout flesh.

Preparation time: 25 minutes
Cooking time: 20–25 minutes
Oven temperature: 180°C, 350°F, Gas Mark 4
To serve: 4

50 g/2 oz butter
2 tablespoons finely chopped shallots
4 medium trout, cleaned but with heads still on
4 large pieces Bayonne ham (Parma ham may be used if more easily available)
150 ml/$\frac{1}{4}$ pint dry white wine
chopped fresh parsley
watercress and thin slices of lemon (optional)

Melt the butter in a large flameproof casserole. Add the shallots and stir until golden. Remove the casserole from the heat.

Wash the trout and pat dry. Wrap each trout in a large piece of the ham. Place the four fish in the casserole, and pour the white wine over. Return to the heat until the wine begins to simmer.

Cover the dish with a tight-fitting lid or, alternatively, a sheet of foil. Bake in the oven for 20–25 minutes or until the trout are just firm. Let the fish cool slightly, then carefully lift them from the casserole to a heated serving platter. Garnish with the parsley and serve.

This is also good cold as a luncheon dish or an elegant first course. If the fish is to be served cold, let it cool in the casserole. Before serving, gently unwrap the ham from each fish, and skin it. This is very easy once the fish is cooked; remove the skin in strips, beginning at the tail and pulling towards the head using a small sharp knife. When all the fish have been skinned, rewrap them in the ham, and serve garnished with watercress and thin slices of lemon.

Truites Bourguignonnes *Trout Cooked in Red Wine*

BURGUNDY

Although it may seem strange to cook trout in red wine, this is an excellent dish.

Preparation time: 15 minutes
Cooking time: 35 minutes
To serve: 6

1 bottle of red Burgundy wine
150 ml/$\frac{1}{4}$ pint water
2 carrots, quartered
2 onions, quartered
1 bouquet garni (bay leaf and fennel, thyme and parsley sprigs)
salt
freshly ground black pepper
6 trout, cleaned and gutted
2 tablespoons finely chopped shallots
175 g/6 oz butter, preferably unsalted
juice of 1 lemon
1 tablespoon finely chopped fresh parsley
1 lemon, sliced, to garnish

Make a court-bouillon by bringing the wine and water to the boil in a saucepan. Add the carrots, onions, bouquet garni and salt and pepper and boil steadily for 15 minutes. The liquid should be reduced by about half.

Rub the insides of the trout with salt and place them side by side in a shallow flameproof casserole or poaching pan. Strain on the boiling court-bouillon and poach the trout very gently for 10 to 15 minutes or until just cooked.

Pour or skim off 150 ml/$\frac{1}{4}$ pint of the court-bouillon and bring rapidly to the boil in a separate saucepan. Boil until reduced by half. Add the shallots and the butter, cut into small pieces, and stir until well combined. Add the lemon juice, adjust the seasoning and sprinkle with the parsley. Pour into a heated sauceboat and keep hot.

Lift the trout onto a heated serving dish, garnish with lemon slices and serve hot, with the sauce.

Poultry

Caneton Aux Navets

Duck with Turnips
MAINE

Duck is eaten so frequently in northern France that it is served in many different ways – sometimes, as in this recipe, braised and surrounded by local vegetables.

Preparation time: 20 minutes
Cooking time: 1¼ hours
Oven temperature: 190°C, 375°F, Gas Mark 5
To serve: 4 to 6

1 large oven-ready duck
salt
freshly ground black pepper
50 g/2 oz butter
150 ml/¼ pint dry white wine
450 ml/¾ pint duck, chicken or veal stock
1 bouquet garni
0.5 kg/1 lb baby turnips, peeled
0.5 kg/1 lb button onions, peeled
1 teaspoon sugar
1 tablespoon flour

Wipe the duck well and prick the skin all over with a sharp-pronged fork. Rub salt and pepper into the skin and into the cavity.

Heat half the butter until foaming in a large flameproof casserole, add the duck and brown it all over. Pour off the fat into another flameproof casserole or heavy saucepan and set aside.

Add the wine to the duck in the first casserole, raise the heat and boil the wine to reduce. Add the stock, return to the boil and add the bouquet garni and salt and pepper to taste. Cover and place in the moderately hot oven, or cook over a low heat on top of the stove so that the liquid is barely simmering, for another 45 to 50 minutes.

Meanwhile, brown the turnips and onions in the butter in the second casserole. Sprinkle with the sugar, season generously, cover and leave to braise over a very low heat for 25 to 35 minutes or until tender.

When the duck is nearly cooked (test by pricking a drumstick with a sharp fork: the liquid which comes out should be just colourless) remove it from the casserole, cut it into serving pieces and keep warm on a deep serving platter. Make a beurre manié by blending the flour with the remaining butter. Add to the liquid in the casserole and stir until smooth. Bring to the boil and simmer for 2 minutes, stirring.

Surround the duck with drained braised vegetables and pour over the sauce just before serving.

Poulet A La Vallée D'Auge

NORMANDY

This dish can be found, with variations, all over Normandy. This version uses all the possible ingredients, but both the apples and the cider can be omitted – the essentials are the Calvados and the crème fraîche.

Preparation time: 20 minutes
Cooking time: about 50 minutes
To serve: 4 to 6

1 tablespoon flour
salt
freshly ground black pepper
1 roasting chicken, jointed, or 4 to 6 chicken joints
100 g/4 oz butter
2 cooking apples, peeled, cored and diced
150 ml/¼ pint Calvados
150 ml/¼ pint cider
150 ml/¼ pint crème fraîche (see page 118)

Chicken with Cream and Apple Brandy

Season the flour generously with salt and pepper and roll the chicken joints in it until they are well coated. Melt the butter in a flameproof casserole. When it is foaming, add the chicken joints and cook them gently – they should only colour to a pale gold. Add the apples and allow to soften.

Pour on the warmed Calvados and set it alight. When the flames have died down, stir in the cider. Cover and continue to simmer very gently until the chicken is cooked.

Stir in the crème fraîche, adjust the seasoning, bring just to the boil and serve.

Note: This is also an excellent way to cook pheasant, as it provides a lot of sauce for what can otherwise be a rather dry bird.

Poulet à la Vallée d'Auge and caneton à la bigarde

Caneton A La Bigarde

Duck with Orange

NORMANDY

Ideally, this should be made with Seville oranges, as their rather bitter flavour adds an aromatic tang to the dish, counteracting the richness of the duck.

Preparation time: 20 minutes
Cooking time: $1\frac{1}{2}$ hours
Oven temperature: 220°C, 425°F, Gas Mark 7; reduced to 190°C, 375°F, Gas Mark 5
To serve: 4 to 6

1 large oven-ready duck, with giblets
1 garlic clove, halved
salt
freshly ground black pepper
1 onion, chopped
1 carrot, chopped
1 bay leaf
finely pared rind and juice of 2 to 3 Seville oranges or 1 sweet Spanish navel orange
25 g/1 oz butter
50 g/2 oz flour
150 ml/$\frac{1}{4}$ pint dry white or red wine
pinch of sugar

Wipe the duck well and rub it, inside and out, with the cut surface of the clove of garlic. Discard the garlic. Rub salt liberally into the skin and prick it all over with a sharp-pronged fork. Put the duck on a rack in a roasting pan and roast for 15 minutes in the hot oven, then lower the temperature and roast for a further $1\frac{1}{4}$ hours, or until the juice that runs out when you pierce the thickest part of the drumstick is clear or just pale pink. Pour off the fat from time to time.

Meanwhile, put the duck giblets, onion, carrot and bay leaf in a saucepan with plenty of water. Bring to the boil and simmer for 1 hour. Strain the stock and reserve 450 ml/$\frac{3}{4}$ pint.

Cut the orange rind into very thin strips. (The rind of two of the Seville oranges is sufficient.) Plunge the strips into boiling water, boil for 3 minutes, then drain. Set aside.

Fifteen minutes before the duck is ready, begin to make the sauce. Melt the butter in a heavy saucepan, and allow to turn nutty brown. Add the flour, stir well and cook over a moderate heat until the mixture is pale caramel brown. Gradually stir in the wine, then add the strained giblet stock. Add the sugar and salt and pepper to taste and simmer over a moderate heat, stirring, until the sauce has thickened.

When the duck is ready, carve it into serving pieces and arrange them on a heated platter. Skim the fat from the juices that remain in the roasting pan and add to the sauce with the juice that has run from the duck when carving. Stir in the orange rind strips and juice. Heat through well and pour over the duck before serving.

Poulet Farci A La Cauchoise *Normandy Stuffed Chicken*

NORMANDY

This method of part braising, part roasting the bird produces a rich and juicy dish.

Preparation time: 30 minutes
Cooking time: 50 minutes to 1 hour
Oven temperature: 220°C, 425°F, Gas Mark 7
To serve: 4 to 6

1 large roasting chicken, with giblets
75 g/3 oz butter
2 onions, finely chopped
2 fresh tarragon branches, finely chopped, or 1 teaspoon dried tarragon
175 g/6 oz sausage meat
1 thick slice of stale white bread
1 egg, lightly beaten
salt
freshly ground black pepper
2 tablespoons Calvados
0.5 kg/1 lb button onions, peeled
450 ml/¾ pint cider
1 bouquet garni

Finely chop the chicken giblets, including the liver. Melt 25 g/1 oz of the butter in a frying pan, add the giblets, chopped onions and tarragon and fry gently, stirring well, until the onions are pale golden. Add the sausage meat and continue cooking, stirring, until all the mixture has changed colour.

Meanwhile, soak the bread in water until softened. Squeeze out all excess moisture.

Turn the cooked sausage meat mixture into a bowl, add the squeezed out bread and the egg and mix well. Season to taste with salt and pepper and use to stuff the chicken. Rub the outside of the chicken with salt and pepper, then truss it.

Melt the remaining butter in a flameproof casserole. When foaming, add the chicken and fry until light golden brown all over. Pour on the warmed Calvados and set alight. When the flames die down, add the button onions and allow them to brown gently. Pour on the cider, add the bouquet garni and a little more salt and pepper and bring to the boil. Cover, lower the heat and simmer for 40 minutes.

Uncover the casserole, place in the oven and allow the top of the chicken to brown. Remove the chicken and onions to a heated serving dish. Discard the bouquet garni and boil the cooking liquid briskly to reduce before serving with the chicken.

Coq Au Vin Au Riesling *Chicken Cooked in Riesling Wine*

ALSACE

This classic Alsatian dish combines the local Riesling wine with the lovely yellow morel mushrooms that are one of the joys of the area, and eaten locally it has an incomparable flavour. A good dry white wine, and field or cultivated mushrooms, will still make a very excellent dish. Serve with noodles or simply a green salad.

Preparation time: 20 minutes
Cooking time: 1 hour 20 minutes
To serve: 4 to 6

1 roasting chicken, jointed, or 4 to 6 chicken joints
salt
freshly ground black pepper
1 tablespoon flour
50 g/2 oz butter
8 shallots, finely chopped
2 tablespoons brandy
300 ml/½ pint Riesling or other white wine
225 g/8 oz morel or other mushrooms, sliced
4 tablespoons crème fraîche (see page 118) or double cream

Season the pieces of chicken and dust them very lightly with the flour. Melt the butter in a flameproof casserole and quickly brown the chicken pieces on all sides. Remove from the casserole and keep warm.

Add the shallots to the casserole and soften. Return the chicken pieces, pour on the brandy and set alight. When the flames have died down, add the wine and the mushrooms. Cover and simmer for about 1 hour, or until the chicken is cooked.

Remove the chicken pieces and arrange on a heated serving dish. Bring the cooking juices to the boil and boil briskly for a few minutes to reduce. Lower the heat. Add the cream and stir to make a smooth sauce. Adjust the seasoning. Pour the sauce carefully over the pieces of chicken to coat them and serve very hot.

Caneton Aux Cerises *Duck with Cherries*

ILE DE FRANCE

The Ile de France used to be known as the garden of Paris, and once the orchards that surrounded it provided the city with all its fruit. This abundance has left its mark on some of the dishes of the classic cuisine, as in this dish which combines the richness of duck with the tart cherries that still grow in Montmorency, on the outskirts of Paris.

Preparation time: 30 minutes
Cooking time: 1¾ hours
Oven temperature: 220°C, 425°F, Gas Mark 7; reduced to 190°C, 375°F, Gas Mark 5
To serve: 4 to 6

1 large oven-ready duck, with giblets
salt
freshly ground black pepper
1 onion, quartered
1 carrot, quartered
1 bouquet garni
0.5 kg/1 lb tart or Morello cherries, stoned
juice of ½ lemon
3 tablespoons brandy or marc
25 g/1 oz sugar
2 tablespoons red wine vinegar
150 ml/¼ pint white wine
40 g/1½ oz butter
25 g/1 oz flour

Wipe the duck well inside and out and season it generously with salt and pepper all over. Prick the skin with a sharp-pronged fork and place in a roasting pan in the hot oven for 15 minutes, then lower the oven temperature to moderately hot and roast for a further 1¼ hours, or until the juice that runs out when you prick the thickest part of the drumstick with a sharp-pronged fork is just clear. Pour off the fat from time to time.

Meanwhile, make a stock by simmering the duck giblets, onion, carrot and bouquet garni in water.

Marinate the cherries in the lemon juice and brandy or marc.

Put the sugar and vinegar into a small heavy saucepan and stir over a moderate heat to dissolve the sugar. Bring to the boil and allow the vinegar to evaporate. Remove from the heat when the mixture is just turning dark brown; do not allow it to burn. Add 150 ml/¼ pint of the strained giblet stock and stir to dissolve the caramel.

When the duck is cooled, carve it into serving pieces and keep warm on a heated serving dish. Pour off excess fat from the roasting pan, add the wine to the pan and bring to the boil, stirring well to amalgamate any sediment. Add the caramelized stock and the marinating liquid from the cherries. Boil rapidly for a few minutes to reduce a little.

Work 25 g/1 oz of the butter with the flour into a beurre manié and add to the sauce. Stir until smooth and simmer until the sauce thickens. Add the last piece of butter to give the sauce a glaze.

Add the cherries to the sauce and allow them to heat through. Pour the sauce carefully over and around the duck and serve very hot.

Poulet A La Comtoise

Chicken with Cheese
FRANCHE-COMTE

The creamily melting cheese of the Franche-Comté makes this a most luxurious dish, while the ingredients are very simple.

Preparation time: 40 minutes
Cooking time: $1\frac{1}{2}$ hours
Oven temperature: 230°C, 450°F, Gas Mark 8
To serve: 6 to 8

1 large roasting chicken, trussed
salt
freshly ground black pepper
150 g/5 oz butter
3 carrots, chopped
2 leeks, white parts only, thinly sliced
2 celery sticks, thinly sliced
about 1.5 litres/$2\frac{1}{2}$ pints boiling water
225 g/8 oz button mushrooms
25 g/1 oz flour
150 ml/$\frac{1}{4}$ pint crème fraîche (see page 118)
1 egg yolk
juice of $\frac{1}{2}$ lemon
pinch of grated nutmeg
100 g/4 oz Comté or Gruyère cheese, grated

Coq au vin au Riesling and poulet à la Comtoise

Wipe the chicken and season well with salt and pepper inside and out. Melt 50 g/2 oz of the butter in a flameproof casserole and when foaming, add the chicken. Cover the pot and let the chicken colour slowly, turning it over frequently, so that it is buttery and uniformly light golden brown all over. Do not let the butter darken. Remove the chicken and set aside.

Add the carrots, leeks and celery to the casserole and cook gently until softened.

Return the chicken to the casserole, placing it on top of the bed of vegetables. Pour on enough boiling water to cover the chicken. Cover and simmer for about 1 hour.

Melt 25 g/1 oz of the butter in a small saucepan and cook the mushrooms for 5 minutes over a quite high heat, so that they do not lose their moisture. Set aside.

When the chicken is cooked, remove it from the casserole, place in an ovenproof dish and keep warm. Strain the cooking liquid and boil very rapidly to reduce to about 900 ml/$1\frac{1}{2}$ pints. Pass the vegetables through a blender or mouli-légumes.

Meanwhile work the flour into the remaining butter to make a beurre manié. Mix the cream into the egg yolk and stir in the lemon juice to make a smooth sauce.

When the stock has reduced sufficiently, strain it again into another clean saucepan and add the vegetable purée. Stir until smooth. Add the beurre manié, a little at a time, until it is all incorporated, and bring briefly to the boil. Remove from the heat and add the egg and cream mixture. Adjust the seasoning and add the nutmeg.

Sprinkle the chicken with half the cheese and press it in firmly. Surround with the mushrooms and gently pour over the sauce, so that the chicken becomes lightly coated as well as surrounded by the sauce. Sprinkle with the remaining cheese and place in the hot oven. Cook for 15 minutes or until the top is golden brown and lightly crusted. Serve straight from the oven and carve at the table.

Oie Braisée A L'Alsacienne *Braised Goose with Sauerkraut*

ALSACE

Goose – roast, braised or preserved – can be found on menus everywhere in Alsace and Lorraine. The sauerkraut in this recipe, which is a typically Alsatian way of cooking goose, counteracts the richness of the bird; duck is also very good cooked in the same way.

Preparation time: 30 minutes
Cooking time: $2\frac{1}{2}$ hours minimum
Oven temperature: 190°C, 375°F, Gas Mark 5
To serve: 8 to 10

1 young oven-ready goose, trussed
salt
freshly ground black pepper
0.5 kg/1 lb pork sausage meat
2 large onions, finely chopped
1.5 kg/3 lb sauerkraut, rinsed and drained
1 bouquet garni (bay leaf and thyme and rosemary sprigs)
12 juniper berries, lightly crushed
0.5 kg/1 lb smoked pork
300 ml/$\frac{1}{2}$ pint white wine
50 g/2 oz butter
1 tablespoon oil

Remove the layers of fat from inside the goose. Season the goose well with salt and pepper inside and out and stuff it with the sausage meat, seasoned to taste.

Melt the goose fat in a large flameproof casserole, add the onions and sauerkraut and turn over a medium heat to coat evenly with a little fat. Add the bouquet garni, juniper berries and a little salt and pepper and bury the piece of smoked pork in the centre. Add half the wine and enough water to come halfway up the sauerkraut. Bring to the boil, cover and simmer for at least $2\frac{1}{2}$ hours, checking from time to time that the mixture is not getting too dry. Add a little water if necessary.

If you have a casserole large enough to hold the goose (or if you are cooking duck in this recipe) melt the butter with the oil in it and brown the goose on all sides. Add the remaining wine, cover and cook over a medium heat for at least 2 hours, or until the goose is cooked.

If the bird is too large to fit into a casserole, brush it with melted fat and cook on a rack in a roasting pan in the oven.

When the goose is cooked, carve it into serving pieces and keep warm. Skim the fat off the cooking juices.

Remove the piece of smoked pork from the casserole and carve it into thick slices.

Pile the sauerkraut into the centre of a heated large, deep serving dish. Surround with the slices of smoked pork, and top with the pieces of goose. Pour on the cooking juices from the goose and serve very hot.

Oie braisée à l'Alsacienne

Faisan A La Vigneronne *Pheasant with Grapes*

BURGUNDY

This is a dish to celebrate the end of the grape harvest.

Preparation time: 30 minutes
Cooking time: about $1\frac{1}{4}$ hours
Oven temperature: 180°C, 350°F, Gas Mark 4
To serve: 4

1 plump pheasant, plucked and trussed
salt
freshly ground black pepper
150 g/5 oz butter
1 carrot, chopped
1 onion, chopped
300 ml/$\frac{1}{2}$ pint Chablis
4 slices of white bread
1 pheasant liver
4 chicken livers
1 tablespoon brandy, warmed
150 ml/$\frac{1}{4}$ pint crème fraiche (see page 118)
100 g/4 oz black grapes, peeled and seeded
100 g/4 oz white grapes, peeled and seeded

Season the pheasant inside and out generously. Melt 50 g/2 oz of the butter in a flameproof casserole, add the pheasant and brown lightly on all sides. Lift it out of the casserole. Spread the carrot and onion on the bottom of the casserole and place the pheasant on top. Moisten with a little of the wine. Cover the casserole and place in the oven. Cook for 45 to 55 minutes, basting from time to time and adding a little more butter if the pheasant seems to be getting too dry.

Melt 50 g/2 oz of the remaining butter in a frying pan and quickly brown the pieces of bread on both sides. Remove and keep warm.

Add the pheasant liver and chicken livers to the pan and cook until they change colour. Pour on the warmed brandy, set alight and leave until the flames die down.

Remove the livers from the frying pan to a cold plate and mash them with a fork. Mash in the remaining butter and spread this mixture on the pieces of fried bread.

When the pheasant is ready, take it out of the casserole and cut into four pieces. Place on a heated serving dish and keep warm. Pour half the remaining wine into the casserole and the other half into the frying pan. Bring to the boil, stirring well to remove any sediment on the bottom. Pour the wine from the frying pan into the casserole, and continue to boil for a few minutes to reduce. Stir in the cream, season to taste with salt and pepper and heat through.

Surround the pheasant with the grapes and the pieces of fried bread. Pour on the sauce and serve very hot.

Coq Au Vin *Chicken Cooked in Red Burgundy Wine*

BURGUNDY

This is one of the classic dishes of French cooking, to be made for Sundays and holidays, using excellent ingredients. Use a large plump roaster or capon, a really good bottle of red Burgundy and some tasty field mushrooms or cèpes.

The dish needs no accompaniment other than a bottle of the wine in which it has been cooked, and it may be followed by a green salad.

Preparation time: 30 minutes
Cooking time: 1 to $1\frac{1}{2}$ hours
To serve: 6 to 8

1 large roasting chicken or capon, jointed, or 6 to 8 chicken joints
2 tablespoons flour
salt
freshly ground black pepper
90 g/$3\frac{1}{2}$ oz butter
100 g/4 oz lean bacon, diced
1 onion, quartered
1 carrot, quartered
4 tablespoons brandy
600 ml/1 pint red Burgundy wine
1 garlic clove, lightly crushed
1 bouquet garni
1 sugar lump
2 tablespoons oil
0.5 kg/1 lb small onions, peeled
pinch of sugar
1 teaspoon wine vinegar
225 g/8 oz button mushrooms
6 slices of white bread, crusts removed

Coat the chicken pieces with 1 tablespoon of the flour, liberally seasoned with salt and pepper.

Melt 25 g/1 oz of the butter in a flameproof casserole, add the bacon, quartered onion and carrot and fry gently until the bacon begins to change colour. Add the chicken pieces, raise the heat and fry until they are golden brown on all sides.

Heat the brandy in a small saucepan, set it alight and pour over the chicken, shaking the pan so that all the chicken pieces are covered in flames. When the flames have subsided, pour on the wine and stir to remove any sediment from the bottom of the casserole. Add the garlic, bouquet garni and sugar lump. Bring to the boil, then cover and simmer very gently until the chicken is tender. Test by pricking the thickest part of a drumstick; the chicken is done when the juice runs out clear.

Meanwhile, melt another 25 g/1 oz of the butter with $\frac{1}{2}$ tablespoon of the oil in a frying pan. Add the small onions and fry until they begin to brown. Add the pinch of sugar and the vinegar, together with 1 tablespoon of the chicken cooking liquid. Cover and simmer for 10 to 15 minutes or until just tender. Keep warm.

Melt 25 g/1 oz of the butter with $\frac{1}{2}$ tablespoon of the oil in a heavy saucepan that is wide enough to hold the mushrooms lying flat. Raise the heat and add the mushrooms. Cook until they are crisp and lightly browned. Keep warm.

When cooked, lift the chicken pieces out of the casserole and place in a deep heated serving dish. Surround with the small onions and mushrooms and keep hot.

Discard the bouquet garni. Skim the excess fat off the cooking liquid and put it into a frying pan. Boil the liquid in the casserole briskly to reduce for 3 to 5 minutes.

Add the remaining oil to the fat in the frying pan and quickly fry the pieces of bread until golden brown on both sides. Cut each slice into triangles.

Work the remaining flour into the remaining butter. Take the casserole off the heat and add the beurre manié in small pieces to the cooking liquid. Stir until smooth, then bring just to the boil. The sauce should now be quite thick and shiny. Adjust the seasoning and pour over the chicken. Garnish with the triangles of fried bread.

Poulet A L'Estragon *Tarragon Chicken*

BURGUNDY

To get the full flavour this dish should only be made with fresh French tarragon.

Preparation time: 20 minutes
Cooking time: 45 to 50 minutes
To serve: 4 to 6

4 to 6 fresh tarragon branches
about 2 teaspoons sea or rock salt
about 1 teaspoon coarsely ground black pepper
1 roasting chicken, jointed, or 4 to 6 chicken joints
75 g/3 oz butter
225 g/8 oz small onions, peeled
½ bottle of dry white wine
1 bouquet garni

Strip the leaves off the tarragon and chop them fairly finely. Mix with the salt and pepper and roll each chicken piece in this mixture, pressing the mixture in quite firmly.

Melt the butter in a wide flameproof casserole and when it is foaming add the chicken pieces. Brown quickly on both sides to a light golden brown. Remove the chicken joints from the casserole and keep warm.

Add the onions to the casserole and brown lightly. Take out and set aside.

Return the chicken pieces to the casserole, as far as possible laying them side by side on the bottom of the casserole, skin side down. Tuck the onions into any spaces between. Pour on the wine and bring to the boil. Add the bouquet garni, cover the casserole and lower the heat so that the liquid is only barely simmering. Cook for 40 to 45 minutes.

Test the chicken by pricking a drumstick with a fork or skewer; the liquid that runs out should be just clear, and the chicken will be moist and tender. Discard the bouquet garni before serving.

Poulet De Bresse Rôti *Roast Bresse Chicken*

BURGUNDY

The yellow maize-fed 'poulets de Bresse' are famous throughout France as the plumpest and tastiest of chickens. This method of roasting shows the care taken by the French housewife with even the simplest process, and produces a moist, tender roast chicken, with crisp, golden brown skin.

Preparation time: 15 minutes
Cooking time: 1 to 1¼ hours
Oven temperature: 220°C, 425°F, Gas Mark 7; reduced to 190°C, 375°F, Gas Mark 5

1 large roasting chicken, with giblets
1 garlic clove, halved
salt
freshly ground black pepper
1 teaspoon dried or finely chopped fresh mixed herbs
100 g/4 oz butter, softened
1 onion, quartered
1 carrot, quartered
1 bouquet garni
strip of lemon rind
1 teaspoon flour

Wipe the chicken inside and out and rub first with the cut surface of the clove of garlic and then with salt and pepper and the herbs. Put a small knob of the butter inside the cavity.

Lay the chicken on its side on a rack in the roasting pan and smear the uppermost side liberally with some of the softened butter. Roast in the hot oven for 15 minutes. Turn the chicken over and rub the side that is now uppermost with half of the remaining butter. Return to the oven. After another 15 minutes roasting, turn it breast up and smear the breast with all but a knob of the remaining butter. Lower the oven temperature and roast for a further 30 to 40 minutes, basting frequently with the fat in the pan.

Meanwhile put the giblets, onion, carrot, bouquet garni and lemon rind in a saucepan, cover with water and bring to the boil. Leave to simmer while the chicken is cooking.

Test to see if the chicken is cooked by piercing the thickest part of the drumstick: the chicken is ready when the juice that runs out is just clear. Remove it to a heated serving platter and keep warm, but do not return to the oven. The chicken should be left for at least 5 minutes, while you make the gravy, before carving.

Pour or skim off any excess fat from the roasting pan and bring the remaining juice to the boil. Strain in 150 ml/¼ pint of the giblet stock and bring rapidly to the boil.

Make a beurre manié by working the flour into the remaining butter and add to the roasting pan off the heat. Stir to make a smooth sauce, adjust the seasoning and bring to the boil. Simmer for 1 minute, then strain into a heated sauceboat to serve with the chicken.

Coq au vin (page 61), poulet de Bresse rôti and poulet à l'estragon

Poulet Basque *Chicken with Pepper and Tomatoes*

BEARN

Ideally, this dish should be made with some *piments basque* which are not quite as hot as chilli peppers, but are a good deal spicier than the ordinary pimiento. If these are not obtainable, add one chilli pepper or paprika.

Preparation time: 20 minutes
Cooking time: 1 hour
To serve: 4 to 6

1 roasting chicken, jointed, or 4 to 6 chicken joints
salt
freshly ground black pepper
50 g/2 oz goose or pork fat, or lard
2 large onions, thinly sliced
4 garlic cloves, finely chopped
0.5 kg/1 lb highly spiced basque or Spanish-type sausage, or salami, in one piece
2 green peppers, cored, seeded and sliced
2 hot red chilli peppers, seeded and sliced, or *1 red pepper, cored, seeded and sliced, and 1 tablespoon paprika*
0.5 kg/1 lb tomatoes, skinned and seeded
225–350 g/8–12 oz long grain rice

Season the chicken pieces with salt and pepper. Melt the fat or lard in a flameproof casserole and brown the chicken pieces quickly on all sides. Remove from the pot and set aside.

Add the onions and garlic to the casserole and sweat until soft. Lay the chicken pieces on top of the vegetables and add enough water to come halfway up the chicken. Bring to the boil, then cover and simmer gently for about 15 minutes.

Add the sausage or salami, green peppers, chillis, or red pepper and paprika, and the tomatoes. Re-cover and simmer until the chicken is tender. Adjust the seasoning.

Just before the chicken is done, cook the rice in boiling salted water for about 10 minutes until almost cooked. Drain and place in a shallow flameproof casserole or heavy saucepan. Pour over some of the chicken cooking liquid and simmer until the rice is tender and has absorbed most of the chicken liquid.

Serve by piling the rice onto a heated deep serving dish, or leave in the casserole in which it has cooked. Lay the pieces of chicken on top, together with the sausage cut into chunks and pour over the vegetable mixture and stock. Serve very hot.

Oie Farcie Aux Pruneaux *Goose Stuffed with Prunes*

GUYENNE

The town of Agen in the centre of the Guyenne is famous for its plums and prunes. These are not only stuffed to make a special confectionery but also used a great deal in cooking savoury dishes. Combined with goose they make an exceptionally rich and delicious meal.

Preparation time: 30 minutes (plus soaking overnight)
Cooking time: 2 to $2\frac{1}{2}$ hours
Oven temperature: 220°C, 425°F, Gas Mark 7; reduced to 180°C, 350°F, Gas Mark 4
To serve: 8

4 to 4.5 kg/9 to 10 lb oven-ready goose, with the diced liver
salt
freshly ground black pepper
0.5 kg/1 lb prunes, soaked overnight
300 ml/$\frac{1}{2}$ pint white wine
40 g/$1\frac{1}{2}$ oz butter
1 tablespoon finely chopped shallots
2 tablespoons port or brandy
100 g/4 oz fresh white breadcrumbs
1 small can pâté de foie (optional)
1 teaspoon flour

Rub the goose inside and out liberally with salt and pepper and prick the skin all over so that the fat runs out easily.

Drain the prunes and put them in a saucepan with the wine. Bring to the boil and simmer for about 10 minutes, or until tender. Drain, reserving the cooking liquid. Stone the prunes and chop finely.

Melt 25 g/1 oz of the butter in a frying pan, add the shallots and fry until softened. Add the goose liver and cook for 3 minutes or until it just begins to change colour. Remove the liver and shallot mixture to a bowl.

Add the port or brandy to the pan and bring quickly to the boil, stirring to loosen any sediment. Pour into the bowl. Stir in the breadcrumbs, pâté de foie, if used, and the prunes. Stuff the goose with this mixture.

Place the goose on a grid in a large roasting pan and put in the centre of the oven. Lower the temperature after 15 minutes and continue to roast, pouring off the fat occasionally.

When the goose is cooked (test by pricking the thickest part of the drumstick with a skewer – the juice that runs out should be just clear) remove to a heated serving dish. Pour or skim off the remaining fat from the roasting pan, leaving the meat juices. Sprinkle in the flour, stir until smooth and cook gently for 1 minute. Add the prune cooking liquid and bring quickly to the boil, stirring well. Taste the sauce for seasoning, and add the remaining butter, cut into small pieces, to give the sauce a glaze. Pour into a heated sauceboat and serve with the goose.

Meats

Carbonnade De Boeuf Flamande *Beef Braised in Beer*

FLANDERS

The influence of Belgium in this part of France makes itself felt in the frequent use of beer in cooking, as in this sustaining dish to be served on cold days, with baked potatoes or noodles.

Preparation time: 20 minutes
Cooking time: $2\frac{1}{2}$ to 3 hours
Oven temperature: 150°C, 300°F, Gas Mark 2
To serve: 6

1 kg/2 lb braising steak, trimmed and cubed
salt
freshly ground black pepper
50 g/2 oz butter or beef dripping
0.5 kg/1 lb onions, sliced
2 tablespoons flour
1 teaspoon brown sugar
1 tablespoon wine vinegar
600 ml/1 pint dark ale or stout
1 bouquet garni

Season the meat generously with salt and pepper. Melt the butter or dripping in a flameproof casserole and quickly brown the pieces of meat on all sides. Remove and set aside.

Add the onions to the casserole, lower the heat and fry until golden brown. Remove from the casserole and set aside.

Sprinkle the flour into the casserole and cook over a moderately high heat, stirring well, until it is dark golden brown. Add the sugar and vinegar, and when the vinegar has evaporated, add the beer slowly, stirring well to loosen any sediment on the bottom of the casserole, and to make a smooth sauce.

Return the meat and onions to the casserole in alternate layers, add the bouquet garni and bring back to the boil. Cover and cook in the oven until the meat is very tender and the sauce has thickened. You can also simmer the carbonnade over a low heat on top of the stove.

Remove the bouquet garni before serving, and serve very hot.

Hochepot *Boiled Beef with Vegetables*

FLANDERS

The authentic recipe for this sturdy country dish includes a piece of pig's head with the ear, but for less robust appetites a piece of the thick end of belly of pork will make a very nice substitute. The sausage should be a really good meaty, uncooked and coarse country sausage, preferably French, but could also be Belgian or German.

Preparation time: 20 minutes
Cooking time: 3 hours
To serve: 6 to 8

25 g/1 oz butter or lard
about 1 kg/2 lb piece of silverside, brisket or flank of beef, boned and rolled
250 ml/8 fl oz water
0.5 kg/1 lb belly of pork, lean end
250 g/generous 8 oz piece of sausage (see above)
6 carrots, peeled or scraped
6 turnips, peeled
6 leeks
1 white cabbage, quartered and cored
$\frac{1}{2}$ teaspoon ground allspice
salt
freshly ground black pepper

Melt the butter or lard in a large flameproof casserole or stewpot and brown the pieces of beef on all sides. Add the water and bring to the boil. Cover and simmer for one hour, add the pork, and continue cooking for another hour. At the end of this time, skim excess fat off the surface of the cooking liquid, and add the sausage, vegetables, allspice and salt and pepper to taste. Cover and simmer for a further hour.

Lift out the meat and sausage and place on a large heated serving dish. Carve them into thick slices. Surround with the vegetables and serve very hot.

Hochepot and carbonnade de bouef flamande

Bière de Garde
de

Boeuf A La Bourguignonne *Beef Stewed in Burgundy Wine*

BURGUNDY

Made with tender Charollais beef and a good Burgundy wine, this is the richest and most satisfying of all the beef casseroles.

Preparation time: 30 minutes
Cooking time: 3 hours
Oven temperature: 150°C, 300°F, Gas Mark 2
To serve: 6 to 8

1.5 kg/3 lb chuck steak or topside, cubed
50 g/2 oz flour
salt
freshly ground black pepper
150 g/5 oz butter
3 tablespoons olive oil
2 tablespoons brandy
1 bottle of red Burgundy wine
100 g/4 oz streaky bacon, finely diced
2 onions, finely chopped
2 carrots, finely chopped
2 garlic cloves, finely chopped
1 bouquet garni (bay leaf and thyme, parsley and fennel sprigs)
0.5 kg/1 lb small onions, peeled
1 teaspoon sugar
1 teaspoon wine vinegar
1 tablespoon water
0.5 kg/1 lb button mushrooms

Coat the cubes of beef in the flour, which has been liberally seasoned with salt and pepper, so that they all become evenly coated. Melt half the butter with the olive oil in a heavy frying pan. When very hot put in just as much of the beef as will cover the bottom of the pan. Fry quickly, turning, until all the beef cubes are golden brown and lightly crusted all over. Remove from the frying pan to a flameproof casserole. Brown the remaining beef cubes in the same way.

Pour the brandy into the frying pan. Stir well to remove any sediment and allow to bubble fiercely for 1 minute. Add as much wine as the pan will hold and bring to the boil. Allow to boil for 1 minute, then pour all the wine over the meat. The liquid should come just level with the meat – add a little water if necessary.

Melt 15 g/½ oz of the butter in the frying pan and quickly fry the bacon, chopped onions, carrots and garlic until just turning golden brown. Add to the casserole, together with the bouquet garni. Cover the casserole and place in the oven, or leave to simmer, half covered, over a very low heat on top of the stove. Cook for 2 hours.

Melt half the remaining butter in the frying pan and quickly brown the small onions. Just as they begin to turn golden brown, sprinkle with the sugar, add the vinegar and water and cook for another minute to allow the moisture to evaporate. Add to the casserole and continue to cook for another hour.

Just before the casserole is ready to serve, cook the mushrooms very quickly in the remaining butter. Add the mushrooms to the casserole and adjust the seasoning before serving.

Entrecôtes Bourguignonnes *Steak Cooked in Red Wine*

BURGUNDY

This dish combines all the best ingredients of the area – the tender beef of the Charollais cattle, the full-bodied red wines and the abundant field mushrooms.

Preparation time: 15 minutes
Cooking time: 15 to 20 minutes
To serve: 4

4 steaks
salt
freshly ground black pepper
100 g/4 oz butter
1 tablespoon oil
1 tablespoon finely chopped shallots
300 ml/½ pint red Burgundy wine
100 g/4 oz mushrooms, thinly sliced
½ tablespoon finely chopped fresh parsley

Season the steaks on both sides. Melt half the butter with the oil in a heavy frying pan. When very hot, add the steaks and cook quickly on both sides according to taste. Remove from the pan and keep hot on a heated serving platter.

Add the shallots to the pan and sweat for a few minutes, until they are soft but not coloured. Add the wine, bring rapidly to the boil and allow to reduce to about half.

Meanwhile melt half the remaining butter in a heavy saucepan, add the mushrooms and cook rapidly until tender. Add the mushrooms to the shallots and bring to the boil again, then remove from the heat. Adjust the seasoning and add the remaining butter, cut into small pieces, to give the sauce a glaze.

Pour the sauce over the steaks, sprinkle with the parsley and serve very hot.

Queue De Boeuf A La Bourguignonne *Oxtail Stewed in Red Wine*

BURGUNDY

True to the French housewifely tradition, no part of the animal is wasted, and oxtail is cooked in numerous ways. This is one of the simplest, and the only extravagant ingredient is a bottle of good Burgundy wine. As it needs such long slow cooking, the dish is not worth making in small quantities.

Preparation time: 30 minutes (plus soaking)
Cooking time: about 4 hours
Oven temperature: 150°C, 300°F, Gas Mark 2
To serve: 8 to 10

2 oxtails, thickly sliced
100 g/4 oz streaky bacon or smoked pork, diced
2 onions, chopped
4 carrots, sliced
1 bouquet garni
salt
freshly ground black pepper
1 bottle of red Burgundy wine
pinch of sugar

Soak the oxtail in cold water for a few hours. Drain well.

Fry the bacon or pork in its own fat in a flameproof casserole. When the fat begins to run, raise the heat, add the pieces of oxtail and brown on all sides. Remove the oxtail and add the onions and carrots to the casserole. Cook until just colouring.

Place the pieces of oxtail on top of the vegetables and add the bouquet garni and salt and pepper to taste.

Bring the wine quickly to the boil with the sugar, then pour over the oxtail in the casserole. Bring to the boil again, cover and place in the oven. Cook until the meat is very tender.

Skim off excess fat from the top of the casserole and adjust the seasoning before serving.

Entrecôtes A La Moutarde *Steak with Mustard Sauce*

BURGUNDY

Nothing could be simpler, or better, than a tender steak, cooked with this deceptively smooth sauce.

Preparation time: 10 minutes
Cooking time: 10 to 15 minutes
To serve: 4

4 steaks
salt
freshly ground black pepper
50 g/2 oz butter
1 tablespoon oil
1 tablespoon Dijon mustard
2 tablespoons crème fraîche (see page 118) or double cream

Season the steaks on both sides. Melt the butter with the oil in a heavy frying pan. When very hot, add the steaks and cook on both sides according to taste. Remove from the pan and keep hot on a heated serving platter.

Add the mustard and cream to the frying pan, stir until smooth and bring just to the boil. Adjust the seasoning, pour over the steaks and serve.

Tournedos Rossini *Steak with Pâté de Foie Gras*

ILE DE FRANCE

An incredibly sumptuous dish, this is said to have been invented by the composer himself. If you were to have it in one of the best Paris restaurants, it would be made not only with foie gras truffé, but would probably come topped with a slice of fresh truffle as well. You can, however, make a perfectly good, slightly less extravagant version yourself, using the best pâté de foie you can, preferably homemade (see page 38).

Preparation time: 10 minutes
Cooking time: 20 to 25 minutes
To serve: 4

4 pieces fillet steak
1 garlic clove, halved
salt
freshly ground black pepper
50 g/2 oz butter
1 tablespoon oil
4 slices of white bread
4 slices of pâté de foie
2 tablespoons white wine
watercress to garnish

Prepare the steaks by rubbing each side with the cut surface of the clove of garlic and salt and pepper.

Melt half the butter with half the oil in a heavy frying pan and quickly brown the slices of bread on both sides. Place each on a heated plate and keep warm.

Add the remaining butter and oil to the frying pan and heat until frothing, then add the steaks. Cook for 6 to 8 minutes on each side, according to how rare you like your steak. Place each steak on top of its croûton of fried bread. Top with a piece of pâté, which should melt a little from the heat of the steak. Keep warm.

Pour the wine into the frying pan and allow to bubble while scraping up any sediment from the bottom of the pan. Pour a little of this sauce over the top of each steak and serve immediately, garnished only with watercress.

Entrecôtes Bourguignonne, entrecôtes à la moutarde, and bouef à la Bourguignonne

Tournedos Rossini, filet de bouef en croute and petits pois à la Française (page 103)

Filet De Boeuf En Croûte

Fillet of Beef in a Pastry Case
ILE DE FRANCE

This dish belongs to the realms of haute cuisine, but it is not difficult to produce at home for special occasions.

Preparation time: 30 minutes (plus pastry)
Cooking time: 30 to 35 minutes
Oven temperature: 220°C, 425°F, Gas Mark 7; reduced to 190°C, 375°F, Gas Mark 5
To serve: 8 or more

about 1 kg/2 lb piece fillet of beef
1 garlic clove, halved
2 tablespoons brandy
salt
freshly ground black pepper
75 g/3 oz butter
1 large mild onion, finely chopped
100 g/4 oz mushrooms, finely chopped
about 400 g/14 oz quantity pâte feuilletée (see page 115) or puff pastry
1 egg yolk
1 tablespoon water

Rub the beef all over first with the cut surface of the clove of garlic, then with 1 tablespoon of the brandy, and then with salt and pepper. Melt half the butter in a heavy frying pan, and when it is foaming, put in the beef and seal it quickly on all sides. Take out and leave to cool.

Add the remaining butter to the pan and cook the onion and mushrooms together until soft. Add the remaining brandy, raise the heat and allow to bubble fiercely until almost all the liquid has evaporated. Leave to cool.

Divide the pastry into two parts, roughly one-third and two-thirds. Roll out the smaller piece to form a rectangle. Line a roasting pan with foil lightly buttered on both sides, and lay the pastry rectangle on top. Spread half the cooled mushroom mixture over the centre, lay the beef on top and cover it with the remaining mushroom mixture.

Roll out the remaining pastry to form a larger rectangle. Place it carefully over the top of the beef and then seal the edges well to make a neat parcel. Decorate with leaves made from leftover scraps of pastry. Brush with the egg yolk mixed with the water. Cook in the hot oven for 20 minutes, then lower the oven temperature to moderately hot and cook for a further 10 to 15 minutes. The pastry should have risen on top and be golden brown. The meat inside should be just cooked *à point*: pale brown on the outside and pink in the centre.

Serve whole, and slice thickly at the table.

Note: If you do not like your beef rare, pre-cook the meat in the hot oven for 10 minutes instead of sealing it in the frying pan.

Boeuf En Daube Provençale *Casserole of Beef with Wine and Herbs*

PROVENCE

This is one of those age-old country recipes which originally would have been taken to the village baker for long slow cooking in his oven after the bread-baking is over. The meat must cook so slowly that it emerges tender enough to be eaten with a spoon, and although the casserole should be sealed, a quite irresistible aroma of wine and herbs will steal out during the course of the cooking.

Preparation time: 30 minutes
Cooking time: 4 to 5 hours
Oven temperature: 140°C, 275°F, Gas Mark 1
To serve: 6 to 8

1 tablespoon olive oil
225 g/8 oz salt pork or streaky bacon, diced
2 onions, sliced
2 carrots, sliced
2 garlic cloves, finely chopped
1 kg/2$\frac{1}{4}$ lb chuck or braising steak, trimmed of fat and cut into large cubes
600 ml/1 pint red wine
2 sprigs each of fresh thyme, rosemary and parsley
1 bay leaf
2 strips of orange rind
3 tomatoes, skinned and roughly chopped
salt
freshly ground black pepper
50 g/2 oz black olives, stoned

Heat the oil in a flameproof casserole, add the salt pork or bacon and fry until transparent. Add the onions, carrots and garlic and continue frying until softened. Raise the heat, add the meat and brown on all sides.

Bring the wine to the boil in a separate saucepan and boil fiercely for 5 minutes. Pour it over the meat and add the herbs, orange rind, tomatoes and salt and pepper to taste. Cover closely with a double thickness of foil and then the lid of the casserole and transfer to the oven. Cook for 4 to 5 hours. Add the olives to the dish 5 minutes before serving.

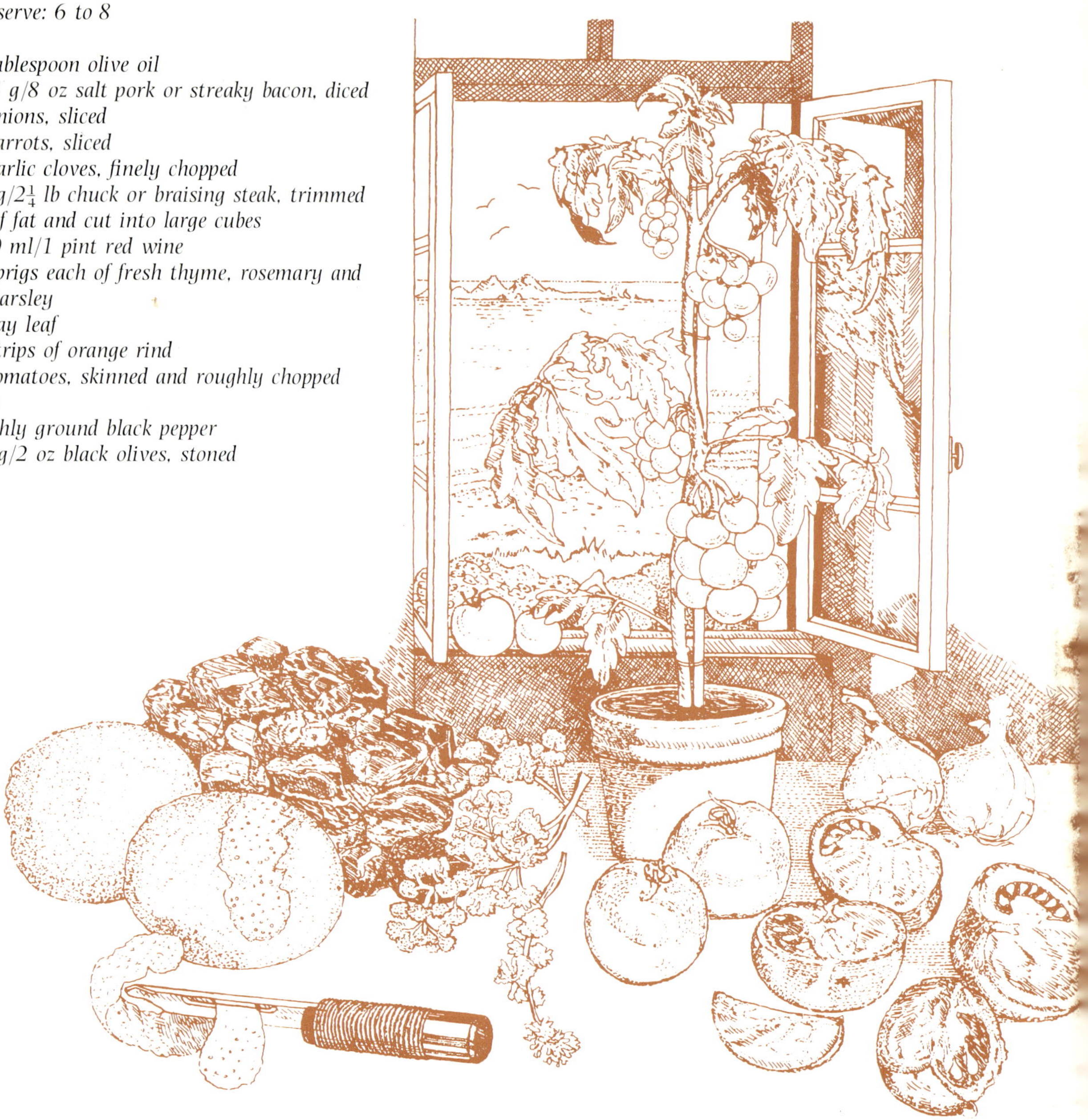

Boeuf A La Mode *Cold Jellied Beef*

ILE DE FRANCE

This is a beautiful dish when carefully made – tender, larded beef in a clear dark jelly, surrounded by bright carrots; the perfect dish for a buffet table, especially as it must be made with a large piece of beef, and has to be made at least a day ahead.

Preparation time: about 40 minutes (plus setting overnight and chilling)
Cooking time: about 5 hours
Oven temperature: 140°C, 275°F, Gas Mark 1
To serve: 12 or more

2.25 to 2.5 kg/5 to 5½ lb piece of rolled, boned beef, such as silverside, top rump or topside
100 g/4 oz piece of pork fat
salt
freshly ground black pepper
½ teaspoon mixed dried herbs
2 garlic cloves, one very finely chopped
50 g/2 oz butter
2 onions, sliced
150 ml/¼ pint brandy
600 ml/1 pint red wine
1 calf's foot or 2 pig's trotters, split and blanched
1 bouquet garni (bay leaf and thyme, rosemary and parsley sprigs)
1 strip of orange rind
1.25 kg/2½ lb carrots
stock or water
a little lemon juice

Garnish
parsley sprigs
lemon slices

If the beef is rolled in fat, remove the outer wrapping of fat. Get the butcher to lard the beef for you, if possible. If not, season the piece of pork fat with plenty of salt and pepper, the herbs and chopped garlic, cut it into strips and use to thread through the meat at intervals using a larding needle.

Melt the butter in a flameproof casserole which is large enough to hold the meat. Add the onions and soften them. Raise the heat, add the piece of meat and brown it quickly on all sides.

Pour in the warmed brandy and set alight. When the flames have died down, pour in the wine. Fit the calf's foot or pig's trotters around the meat, add the bouquet garni, some more seasoning, the orange rind, the whole garlic clove and one carrot cut in half. Add enough stock or water just to cover the meat. Bring to the boil.

Remove from the heat and cover the pot with a very well-fitting lid. Seal the lid with a flour and water paste. Transfer the casserole to the oven and leave to cook for 4 to 5 hours, depending on the size of the meat.

Take the casserole out of the oven and leave to cool a little. Unseal the lid and lift out the meat. It should not have lost its shape but should be very tender. Transfer the meat to another dish, cover well and refrigerate overnight.

Strain the stock and taste it for seasoning. Refrigerate overnight. The calf's foot or pig's trotters may be eaten now on their own.

The next day, remove the lid of fat that will have set on top of the stock. The stock underneath should have set to a light jelly. If it has not set sufficiently, it may be boiled for some minutes to reduce; a little gelatine can also be used to help the setting, but usually this is not necessary. Melt down the jellied stock and add a little lemon juice and more seasoning if necessary. Leave to cool.

Cook the remaining carrots, left whole if they are young and small, cut lengthwise into halves or quarters if not, in boiling salted water until just tender. Drain and cool.

Slice the meat thickly – although very tender, it should be possible to slice it neatly with a really sharp carving knife once the meat has been chilled and left to set overnight. Arrange the slices of meat in a large serving dish, at least 5 cm/2 inches deep. Surround with the carrots. When the stock is cool but has not yet begun to set, pour it carefully over the meat and carrots. Chill for several hours until set before serving, garnished with sprigs of parsley and slices of lemon.

Carbonnade Nîmoise

Lamb Baked with Potatoes and Aubergines
LANGUEDOC

This is an economical and filling dish from the Languedoc, an area that is perhaps less exuberant in its cooking than Provence, but famous for several of the more substantial dishes of the classic French *cuisine bourgeoise*. The proportion of meat to vegetables, and of the vegetables to each other, can be adjusted to suit individual appetites and what is available: it is the long slow cooking of meat and vegetables together which gives the dish its comforting richness of flavour.

Preparation time: 30 minutes (plus 1 hour for draining aubergines)
Cooking time: 3 hours
Oven temperature: 230°C, 450°F, Gas Mark 8; reduced to 180°C, 350°F, Gas Mark 4
To serve: 6 to 8

1 kg/2 lb aubergines, diced
salt
1 leg of lamb, boned and cut into 1 cm/$\frac{1}{2}$ inch thick slices
2 garlic cloves, cut into slivers
freshly ground black pepper
2 tablespoons olive oil
100 g/4 oz bacon or salt pork, diced
1 kg/2 lb potatoes, peeled and diced
1 teaspoon dried thyme
1 teaspoon dried marjoram

Put the aubergines in a colander, sprinkle liberally with salt and leave to drain for 1 hour.

Spike each lamb steak with one or two slivers of garlic. Season the lamb steaks on both sides with salt and pepper.

When the aubergines are ready, rinse them, squeeze out well and pat dry.

Heat the oil in a large roasting pan or large flat baking or gratin dish. Scatter on the bacon or salt pork and lay the lamb steaks on top. Cover with the potatoes and aubergines. Sprinkle on a little more salt and pepper and the herbs and place in the oven.

After 20 minutes baking, cover the pan or dish tightly with a double thickness of foil and lower the oven temperature. Cook for at least a further $2\frac{1}{2}$ hours. The dish may be left longer if convenient. Both meat and vegetables should be very tender, and all the liquid absorbed.

Serve hot.

Carbonnade Nimoise and bouef en daube Provençale (page 72)

Gigot A La Couronne D'Ail

Leg of Lamb with a Crown of Garlic
CHARENTE

Recipes using the legendary *quarante gousses d'ail* appear all over the southern part of France where garlic grows in rich abundance. Garlic is sometimes served as a vegetable in its own right, especially in the summer when the crowns are first lifted, the skin is still moist and pliable and the cloves green tinged, fat and juicy.
This dish belongs to the coastal areas where the lambs feed on the reclaimed salt marshes, and garlic is grown. It must be made with the new season's garlic.

Preparation time: 20 minutes
Cooking time: $1\frac{1}{2}$ to 2 hours
Oven temperature: 220°C, 425°F, Gas Mark 7; reduced to 190°C, 375°F, Gas Mark 5
To serve: 6 to 8

40 or more garlic cloves
1 leg of lamb
4 tablespoons olive oil
1 teaspoon dried thyme
1 teaspoon dried rosemary
salt
freshly ground black pepper
150 ml/$\frac{1}{4}$ pint stock
juice of $\frac{1}{2}$ lemon
50 g/2 oz butter

Peel three of the garlic cloves and cut them into slivers. Using a sharp, pointed knife, make small incisions into the surface of the leg of lamb and insert a sliver of garlic in each. Place the lamb in a roasting pan.

Mix the olive oil with the herbs and salt and pepper and pour a little of the mixture over the leg of lamb. Place in the hot oven and after 15 minutes roasting, lower the temperature and baste the lamb with the remaining oil mixture. Continue roasting until the lamb is cooked, basting from time to time. The lamb should be still pink towards the centre. Test by inserting a skewer – the lamb is cooked when the liquid which runs out is only just colourless.

Meanwhile, blanch the remaining garlic cloves, unpeeled, in boiling salted water for 10 minutes. Drain and place in a small saucepan with the stock. Bring to the boil and simmer gently for 20 minutes.

When the lamb is cooked, remove it from the roasting pan and place on a heated serving dish. Surround with the drained garlic cloves. Add the liquid in which the garlic has been simmering to the roasting juices in the pan and bring to the boil, stirring well to loosen any sediment. Season to taste with salt and pepper and add the lemon juice. Stir in the butter cut into small pieces to give the sauce a glaze, pour over the lamb and serve.

Gigot De Pré-Salé Aux Haricots Verts

Roast Lamb with Green Beans and Potatoes
BRITTANY

The salt meadows (*prés-salés*) of Northern Brittany, around St Malo, are grazing grounds for the tender and delicately flavoured lambs famous throughout France. A gigot, or roast leg of lamb, is usually served surrounded with local vegetables, and is always cooked to the point where it is still just pink and very juicy.

Preparation time: 30 minutes
Cooking time: about 1 hour
Oven temperature: 190°C, 375°F, Gas Mark 5
To serve: 6 to 8

1.5 kg/3½ lb leg of lamb
salt
freshly ground black pepper
2 garlic cloves, cut into slivers
175 g/6 oz butter
0.75 kg/1½ lb potatoes, peeled and chopped
1 kg/2 lb French beans, stringed
120 ml/4 fl oz white wine
120 ml/4 fl oz water
2 tablespoons capers
12 juniper berries, roughly chopped

Rub the leg of lamb all over with salt and pepper, then spike it with the slivers of garlic. Place it in a roasting pan. Melt 50 g/2 oz of the butter and pour it over the lamb. Roast in the oven, basting from time to time, for about 1 hour.

After 30 minutes, melt 75 g/3 oz of the butter in a heavy frying pan. When foaming, add the potato slices and turn well so that they each become coated with butter. Add salt and pepper to taste, then lower the heat, cover the pan and cook gently for 30 to 35 minutes or until tender. Stir occasionally to prevent the slices sticking.

When the lamb has been cooking for about 40 minutes, plunge the beans into a large saucepan of boiling salted water and cook rapidly, uncovered, for 15 to 20 minutes or until tender. Drain and keep warm.

After 1 hour, test the lamb to see if it is cooked by pricking with a skewer – it is ready when the liquid which spurts out is just colourless. Remove from the roasting pan and place on a heated deep serving dish. Keep warm.

Pour off the excess fat from the roasting pan. Add a little of the fat to the potatoes and raise the heat to brown them. Add the wine to the juices in the roasting pan. Bring quickly to the boil, scraping well to loosen any sediment. Stir in the water and bring back to the boil. Pour over the lamb.

Mix the capers and juniper berries into the potatoes and arrange them around the lamb alternately with the beans. Dot the beans with the remaining butter just before serving.

Epaule D'Agneau Aux Noix *Shoulder of Lamb with Walnuts*

MARCHE AND LIMOUSIN

Walnut trees grow to mature splendour in this part of France and walnuts and walnut oil are used a great deal in savoury cooking, as well as for cakes and confectionery. They flavour vegetables, sausages and stuffings.

Preparation time: 20 minutes
Cooking time: 1¼ to 1½ hours
Oven temperature: 220°C, 425°F, Gas Mark 7; reduced to 190°C, 375°F, Gas Mark 5
To serve: 4 to 6

1 shoulder of lamb, boned
1 garlic clove, halved
salt and freshly ground black pepper
50 g/2 oz butter
1 onion, finely chopped
225 g/8 oz belly of pork, skinned, boned and finely minced, or *sausage meat*
8 walnuts, shelled and chopped
2 tablespoons finely chopped fresh parsley
finely grated rind of 1 orange
1 egg, beaten
150 ml/¼ pint white wine

Rub the shoulder inside the cavity and on the outside with the cut surface of the garlic clove and season well with salt and pepper.

Melt half the butter in a frying pan, add the onion and fry until softened. Add the pork or sausage meat and fry very quickly until the meat just begins to change colour.

Turn out into a bowl, add the walnuts, parsley, orange rind and salt and pepper to taste and bind the mixture with the egg. Stuff into the cavity in the shoulder of lamb left by the bone. Place the shoulder on a rack in a roasting pan, dot with the remaining butter and place in the hot oven.

After 15 minutes roasting, lower the oven temperature and continue to roast, basting from time to time, until the meat is cooked. Test by inserting a skewer: the juice that runs out should be only just colourless, and the meat should be pink but set in the centre.

Place the meat on a heated serving dish and keep warm. Add the wine to the roasting pan and bring quickly to the boil, stirring well to loosen any sediment. Season to taste with salt and pepper and pour into a heated sauceboat. Serve the meat very hot, and slice at the table.

Navarin Printanier

Lamb Cooked with Spring Vegetables
BERRY

Paris is usually the first to enjoy the primeurs, the delicate young spring vegetables brought in from nearby market gardens at the peak of tender, youthful perfection. Bunches of bright orange carrots with frilly green foliage, pink-flushed baby turnips, waxy yellow new potatoes no bigger than a hen's egg, and juicy young peas – as soon as these arrive in the vegetable stalls, it is time to make a navarin.

Preparation time: 30 minutes
Cooking time: 1 to 1¼ hours
To serve: 6 to 8

50 g/2 oz butter
2 onions, thinly sliced
2 garlic cloves, finely chopped
1 shoulder of lamb, boned and cut into cubes
2 tablespoons flour
1 teaspoon sugar
600 ml/1 pint stock or water
1 bouquet garni
salt
freshly ground black pepper
0.5 kg/1 lb new potatoes, scrubbed or scraped
0.5 kg/1 lb young carrots, scrubbed or scraped
0.5 kg/1 lb small onions, peeled
0.5 kg/1 lb baby turnips, scrubbed
0.5 kg/1 lb shelled peas

Melt the butter in a flameproof casserole, add the sliced onions and garlic and fry until golden brown. Remove from the casserole.

Add the meat to the casserole and fry quickly, stirring to brown on all sides. Remove from the casserole.

Sprinkle the flour and sugar into the casserole and stir until it becomes dark brown, but not burnt. Add the stock or water slowly, stirring well, to obtain a smooth sauce.

Return the meat and onions to the casserole with the bouquet garni and salt and pepper to taste. Cover and simmer for 20 minutes.

Add the potatoes and carrots to the casserole. Re-cover and simmer for a further 10 minutes.

Add the small onions and turnips and continue to simmer, covered, for another 15 minutes.

Add the peas, raise the heat a little and cook, uncovered, until the peas are tender (about 10 minutes). The meat and all the other vegetables should be ready at about the same time – they must not be allowed to overcook and lose their shape. The sauce should be smooth and quite thin, but if it seems to be at all watery, you can add a little beurre manié – (a blended paste of flour and butter) to thicken it at the end. Adjust the seasoning before serving.

Jambon Persillé *Ham in Aspic*

BURGUNDY

One of the prettiest sights in the *charcuterie* windows in the Burgundy area, especially around Easter time, is the marbled pink and green jambon persillé, usually sold out of large white china bowls.

It is not worth making this dish in small quantities, but it is not difficult to prepare and is lovely on a summer table.

Preparation time: 30 minutes (plus setting overnight)
Cooking time: 4 hours minimum
To serve: 10 to 12

1.5 to 2 kg/3 to 4½ lb piece 'green' bacon, gammon or hock, soaked in cold water overnight if necessary
2 calf's feet or pig's trotters
1 large bouquet garni (bay leaves and parsley, thyme and tarragon sprigs)
12 peppercorns
2 onions, quartered
1 bottle of mersault or other dry white wine
2 teaspoons white wine vinegar
salt
freshly ground black pepper
100 g/4 oz fresh parsley, finely chopped

Put the bacon into a large saucepan, cover with cold water and bring very slowly to the boil. Pour off the water and rinse the pan and bacon. Cover with cold water again and bring slowly to the boil. Simmer for 1 hour.

Drain and rinse the bacon. When the bacon is cool enough to handle, remove the rind if necessary and cut the meat off the bone into large pieces.

Blanch the calf's feet or trotters in boiling water and drain.

Put the bacon pieces back into the clean saucepan, add the calf's feet or trotters, the bouquet garni, peppercorns, onions and wine. Add enough water to cover the meat. Bring slowly to the boil, then simmer for about 3 hours or until the meat is very tender. Skim any fat or scum off the cooking liquid from time to time.

When the bacon is ready, lift it out of the saucepan. Strain the cooking liquid into another bowl. Add the vinegar to the liquid and adjust the seasoning. Leave to cool.

Mash the bacon lightly with a fork and put into a large serving dish, preferably white to show off the pink and green of the finished dish.

When the cooking liquid begins to set into a jelly, skim off any fat that may have risen to the surface and stir in the parsley. Pour over the bacon and leave to set overnight in the refrigerator.

You can serve the dish in its bowl or turn it out onto a platter.

Saupiquet Nivernais *Smoked Ham in Cream Sauce*

NIVERNAIS

Recipes for a saupiquet (from the verb meaning to spike with salt) can be traced back as far as the 16th century. This dish is quite sharp, especially if using smoked ham, so serve with boiled or mashed potatoes.

Preparation time: 25 minutes
Cooking time: 25 minutes
To serve: 4

100 g/4 oz butter
4 good slices of smoked or cooked ham
50 g/2 oz flour
150 ml/¼ pint stock or water
150 ml/¼ pint white wine
4 tablespoons wine vinegar
1 tablespoon finely chopped shallots
6 peppercorns, lightly crushed
6 juniper berries, lightly crushed
300 ml/½ pint crème fraîche (see page 118)
salt
freshly ground black pepper
finely chopped fresh tarragon or parsley to garnish

Melt 90 g/3½ oz of the butter in a large frying pan, add the pieces of ham and quickly sear on both sides. Remove from the pan and keep hot on a heated serving platter.

Sprinkle the flour into the pan and cook, stirring, until the mixture begins to turn brown. Gradually stir in the stock or water then the wine. Stir until smooth, then bring to the boil and cook gently for 1 minute.

Put the vinegar into a small saucepan together with the shallots, peppercorns and juniper berries and bring quickly to the boil. Boil until reduced by half, then strain into the sauce in the frying pan. Add the cream to the sauce and stir until very smooth. Adjust the seasoning.

Add the remaining butter, cut into small pieces, to give the sauce a glaze. Pour the sauce over the slices of ham, sprinkle with the tarragon or chives and serve hot.

Saupiquet Nivernaise and jambon persillé

Noisettes De Porc Aux Pruneaux De Tours Pork Chops with Prunes

TOURAINE

The Touraine is famous for its plump and juicy prunes, and Tours itself for the richness of its food. This sumptuous dish, which is a speciality of the town, is a feast to be eaten at leisure. It really should be made with the local petillant white Vouvray wine, but any good dry white wine will do. Do not expect to eat more than a little fruit to follow.

Preparation time: 20 minutes (plus soaking)
Cooking time: 30 to 45 minutes
To serve: 6 to 8

225 g/8 oz prunes
½ bottle of white Vouvray
6 to 8 pork escalopes or pork loin chops, boned
1 tablespoon flour
salt
freshly ground black pepper
50 g/2 oz butter
1 tablespoon redcurrant jelly
300 ml/½ pint crème fraîche (see page 118)
squeeze of lemon juice

Soak the prunes in the wine for several hours, then simmer them very gently in the wine until soft. Drain the prunes, reserving the wine. Stone and chop them roughly.

Coat the pork in the flour which has been liberally seasoned with salt and pepper. Melt the butter in a deep frying pan and when it is frothing, add the pork. Cook over a moderate heat, turning once, until just golden on both sides but not browned. Add a tablespoon or two of the prune wine, cover and cook over a gentle heat until the pork is cooked – from 15 to 20 minutes, depending on the thickness of the cuts. When the pork is cooked, transfer it to a heated serving dish.

Add the remaining prune wine to the frying pan, stir well to remove any sediment and bring to the boil. Boil to reduce to a thin syrupy consistency. Add the redcurrant jelly and stir until melted, then add the crème fraîche little by little, stirring to amalgamate. Bring to the boil and boil until quite thick. Add the lemon juice and the prunes and allow them to heat through.

Adjust the seasoning and pour the sauce over the pork in the dish. Serve very hot.

Côtelettes De Porc Au Cidre Pork Chops in Cider

NORMANDY

A simple country dish, this uses the age-old combination of pork and apples. Although pork is not eaten a great deal in Normandy, when it is, it is almost always cooked with apples or with cider, if not both.

Preparation time: 10 minutes
Cooking time: 40 minutes
To serve: 6

6 pork chops, trimmed of excess fat
1 garlic clove, halved
salt
freshly ground black pepper
25 g/1 oz butter or pork dripping
1 tablespoon flour
150 ml/¼ pint cider
2 tablespoons water
1 fresh rosemary sprig
1 tablespoon crème fraîche (see page 118) or double cream

Rub the pork chops all over with the cut surface of the clove of garlic, then season generously on both sides with salt and pepper. Discard the garlic. Melt the butter or dripping in a deep frying pan and quickly brown the chops on both sides. Remove and set aside.

Sprinkle the flour into the pan and stir well. Allow to brown. Gradually stir in the cider and bring to the boil, stirring well and scraping any sediment off the bottom of the pan. Add the water and simmer for 1 minute. Return the chops to the pan with the rosemary, heat, cover and simmer for about 30 minutes or until the chops are cooked.

Stir the crème fraîche into the sauce and adjust the seasoning before serving.

Pieds De Porc St Ménéhould *Grilled Pig's Trotters*

CHAMPAGNE

Pig's trotters, cooked and breadcrumbed, can often be seen in *charcuterie* windows in this part of northern France. The town of St Ménéhould prides itself on its speciality of trotters that have been cooked for such a long time that they can be eaten, bones and all. It is almost impossible to achieve this degree of tenderness at home, but these crispy grilled trotters make an excellent and economical hors d'oeuvre.

Preparation time: 20 minutes
Cooking time: 5½ to 6½ hours
Oven temperature: 220°C, 425°F, Gas Mark 7
To serve: 6

6 pigs trotters
2 onions, peeled
4 cloves
2 carrots, peeled
1 bouquet garni (2 bay leaves and large bunches of thyme, rosemary and parsley)
salt
150 ml/¼ pint wine vinegar
50 g/2 oz butter, softened
75 g/3 oz fine dry white breadcrumbs

Scrub and, if necessary, singe the trotters. Either wrap them in a muslin bag or tie them up well so that they do not lose their shape in the long slow cooking. Put them in a large saucepan together with the onions stuck with the cloves, the carrots, bouquet garni, some salt and the vinegar. Cover with plenty of cold water and bring to the boil. Cover the pan and simmer for 5 to 6 hours, by which time the trotters should be very tender. Drain and leave until cool enough to be handled.

Brush each trotter with the butter, then roll in the breadcrumbs, pressing them in well. Lay in a shallow roasting pan and heat through for 15 minutes in the hot oven. Finish off under a hot grill, so that the outside becomes very crisp and just short of charred.

Serve very hot, with mustard and gherkins, or a vinaigrette or tartare sauce.

Côtes De Porc Savoyarde *Pork Chops with Cabbage and Cheese*

SAVOIE

This is an unusual, satisfying, all-in-one dish.

Preparation time: 20 minutes
Cooking time: 50 minutes to 1 hour
Oven temperature: 190°C, 375°F, Gas Mark 5
To serve: 4

1 savoy cabbage, cored and shredded
65 g/2½ oz butter
1 onion, finely chopped
1 garlic clove, finely chopped
salt
freshly ground black pepper
4 juniper berries, crushed
4 pork chops
300 ml/½ pint white wine
1 tablespoon fine dry white breadcrumbs
1 tablespoon finely grated Gruyère cheese

Blanch the cabbage in boiling salted water for 3 minutes. Drain well. Melt 25 g/1 oz of the butter in a frying pan, add the onion and garlic and fry until softened. Add the cabbage, season lightly with salt and pepper and stir in the juniper berries. Remove from the pan and set aside.

Season the chops on both sides with salt and pepper. Melt another 25 g/1 oz of butter in the pan and, when sizzling, quickly brown the chops on both sides.

Put half the cabbage mixture into an ovenproof dish, lay the pork chops on top, side by side, and cover with the remaining cabbage.

Pour the wine into the frying pan and bring quickly to the boil, stirring to amalgamate any sediment left in the pan. Boil fiercely for 1 minute, then pour over the cabbage. Sprinkle on the breadcrumbs mixed with the cheese, dot with the remaining butter and cook in the oven for 40 minutes, or until golden brown.

Chou Farci D'Auvergne *Stuffed Cabbage Casserole*

AUVERGNE

A good peasant dish to keep out the cold, this is not elegant, but very delicious. Gherkins may be served separately with this dish, and mustard is usually put on the table, too.

Preparation time: 30 minutes
Cooking time: 2½ hours
To serve: 6 to 8

1 large cabbage
3 onions, 1 whole and 2 finely chopped
2 garlic cloves, finely chopped
225 g/8 oz sausage meat
100 g/4 oz bacon, finely diced
100 g/4 oz stale white bread, moistened with water and squeezed dry
1 tablespoon finely chopped fresh herbs – parsley, tarragon or chives
salt
freshly ground black pepper
2 eggs, beaten
0.5 kg/1 lb piece of beef
225 g/8 oz smoked pork or bacon, in one piece
2 leeks, chopped
1 bouquet garni
0.5 kg/1 lb carrots, peeled
0.75 kg/1½ lb potatoes, peeled

Peel off about 10 large outer leaves from the cabbage and plunge them into boiling salted water. Blanch for 5 minutes, then drain well. Mix the chopped onions and garlic into the sausage meat. Add the bacon, bread, herbs and salt and pepper to taste. Bind with the eggs.

Lay the cabbage leaves flat in a straight line, overlapping them closely. Spread the stuffing mixture along the centre, then wrap the leaves right round to make a fat sausage shape. Tie up securely with thread. Place in a large saucepan, together with the beef and the smoked pork or bacon and cover with cold water. Bring very slowly to the boil, skimming off the scum that rises. Add the whole onion, leeks and bouquet garni, together with a little salt and pepper, bearing in mind that the smoked pork may be quite salty. Simmer very gently for about 1½ hours.

Add the carrots and potatoes and continue to simmer for a further 30 minutes. Add the cabbage heart, quartered and cored, and continue to simmer until tender.

Lift out the pieces of meat and stuffed cabbage. Slice meat thickly and arrange on a heated serving platter. Surround with the carrots and potatoes, moisten with a little of the broth and serve very hot. (The remaining broth with its vegetables may be used to make a soup.)

Saucisses Aux Pommes *Pork Sausages Cooked with Apples*

ALSACE

A family dish, this uses the plump, highly seasoned pork sausages, bursting with coarsely chopped meat, in which this area excels. This method of cooking sausages with apples, which mellows the flavour, betrays the German influence on Alsatian cooking.

Preparation time: 15 minutes
Cooking time: 20 to 25 minutes
To serve: 6

6 large, meaty pork sausages
25 g/1 oz butter
1 kg/2 lb cooking apples, peeled, cored and thinly sliced
salt
freshly ground black pepper

Prick the sausages in several places to prevent them from bursting. Melt the butter in a heavy deep frying pan and add the sausages. Brown them quickly all over.

Add the apples to the pan, lower the heat, cover and cook over a gentle heat until the sausages are cooked. The apples should have reduced down to a savoury purée.

Pâté De Pâques Berrichon *Berry Easter Pie*

BURGUNDY

This is the traditional Burgundy meat pie, which at Easter is made with hard-boiled eggs in the centre and in a coffin shape. It can also be made as a round pie.

Preparation time: 40 minutes (plus marinating and making pastry)
Cooking time: 1½ hours
Oven temperature: 180°C, 350°F, Gas Mark 4
To serve: 10 to 12

0.5 kg/1 lb lean pork, roughly chopped
0.5 kg/1 lb lean veal, roughly chopped
2 tablespoons brandy
150 ml/¼ pint white wine
salt
freshly ground black pepper
pinch of ground allspice
pinch of grated nutmeg
pinch of cayenne
2 tablespoons finely chopped fresh parsley
1 quantity pâte brisée (see page 114)
4 hard-boiled eggs, shelled
2 bay leaves
1 small egg
1 tablespoon water

Put the meat in a bowl with the brandy, wine, salt and pepper and the spices. Leave to marinate in a cool place for a few hours.

Drain the meat and mince it coarsely. Moisten with the marinade, add the parsley and mix well. Fry a little pat of the mixture to taste for seasoning.

Roll out two-thirds of the dough to a rectangle about 5 mm/¼ inch thick. Spread on half the meat mixture, leaving a 5 cm/2 inch margin. Lay the hard-boiled eggs on top and cover with the remaining meat. Lay the bay leaves on top. Bring up the sides of the dough rectangle to make flat, perpendicular sides, and form triangle shaped ends to resemble a coffin.

Roll out the remaining dough to form a lid, and pinch the moistened edges together to seal well. Decorate with dough leaves and cut a vent in the top.

Place on a baking sheet and brush all over with the egg lightly beaten with the water. Bake in the oven.

Serve cold, or just slightly warm.

Côtes de porc Savoyarde (page 81), chou farci d'Auvergne and escalopes de veau Chambery (page 85)

Baeckenhofe *Lamb, Pork and Beef Baked with Potatoes*

ALSACE

This northern cousin of the better-known cassoulet of the south is the perfect dish for cold weather. As it needs such long slow cooking (it used to be carried to the baker's, and left in his oven overnight), it is only worth making in large quantities, but it reheats well, so you can make two meals at one time. If you can use mutton instead of lamb, it will give the dish even more flavour.

Preparation time: 30 minutes (plus marinating overnight)
Cooking time: 4 hours minimum
Oven temperature: 150°C, 300°F, Gas Mark 2
To serve: 10 to 12

0.5 kg/1 lb boned shin or shoulder of pork, cut into cubes
0.5 kg/1 lb boned shoulder of mutton or lamb, cut into cubes
0.5 kg/1 lb braising steak, cut into cubes
0.5 kg/1 lb onions, thinly sliced into rings
4 cloves
2 garlic cloves, peeled
1 bouquet garni
450 ml/¾ pint white wine
salt
freshly ground black pepper
butter
1 kg/2 lb potatoes, peeled and thinly sliced

Put all the meat into a large bowl, add one of the onions stuck with the cloves, the garlic cloves, the bouquet garni, wine and plenty of salt and pepper and leave to marinate overnight.

The next day butter a large ovenproof casserole, preferably earthenware. Put in a layer of potatoes, and sprinkle with a little salt and pepper. Add a layer of the drained meat and cover with a layer of onions. Repeat, ending with a layer of potatoes. Pour on the strained marinade.

Cover the casserole and seal the lid with a little flour and water paste. Cook in the oven for at least 4 hours. Serve straight from the oven and break the seal at the table, so that everyone can enjoy the full aroma.

Choucroûte Alsacienne *Braised Sauerkraut with Pork*

ALSACE

A hearty dish for hearty eaters, this is not worth making in small quantities, especially as it is every bit as good reheated. The exact proportion of meat and sausages is not important and will depend on what is available at your local delicatessen, but all the meat must be pork-based.

Preparation time: 30 minutes
Cooking time: 2½ hours
Oven temperature: 180°C, 350°F, Gas Mark 4
To serve: 10 to 12

50 g/2 oz pork, duck or goose fat
1.75 kg/4 lb sauerkraut, rinsed and drained
4 onions, peeled
8 cloves
3 carrots, peeled
2 cooking apples, peeled, cored and chopped
freshly ground black pepper
12 juniper berries
0.5 kg/1 lb smoked bacon or pork
1 knuckle of ham
450 ml/¾ pint white wine
1 large garlic sausage
10 spiced pork sausages
10 frankfurters or similar sausages

Melt the fat in a large flameproof casserole, add the sauerkraut, the onions stuck with the cloves, the carrots and apples. Sprinkle over pepper to taste and the juniper berries, then bury the piece of smoked bacon or pork and the knuckle of ham in the centre. Add the wine and enough water just to come to the top of the sauerkraut. Cover and simmer on top of the stove or in the oven for 1 hour.

Add the garlic and pork sausages, bury them also in the middle of the sauerkraut mixture and continue to cook for another hour. Top up with a little water from time to time if necessary to prevent the choucroûte from sticking on the bottom.

Add the frankfurters and cook for a further 30 minutes.

To serve, discard the onions and carrots and pile the sauerkraut in the centre of a large heated serving dish. Carve the smoked bacon or pork and the ham into thick pieces and lay these down the centre of the dish. Surround with the sausages.

Escalopes De Veau Chambéry *Veal Escalopes with Vermouth*

SAVOIE

Chambéry, once the seat of the Dukes of Savoy, is a picturesque city and the home of the excellent dry vermouth that bears its name and that gives this dish its subtle flavour.

Preparation time: 5 minutes
Cooking time: 15 minutes
To serve: 4

4 veal escalopes
salt
freshly ground black pepper
lemon juice
50 g/2 oz butter
5 tablespoons dry vermouth
150 ml/¼ pint crème fraîche (see page 118)

Season the escalopes liberally on both sides with salt, pepper and lemon juice. Melt the butter in a heavy frying pan and when foaming add the escalopes. Fry them quickly until just golden brown on both sides. Remove from the pan and keep hot.

Add the vermouth to the pan and stir well to loosen any sediment. Bring quickly to the boil and boil for 1 minute to reduce. Add the crème fraîche and stir until smooth. Bring just to the boil.

Adjust the seasoning, then return the escalopes to the pan and simmer for 1 minute to allow the meat to heat through and the sauce to thicken a little. Serve very hot.

Escalopes De Veau Au Calvados *Veal Escalopes with Apple Brandy*

NORMANDY

This is a dish for special occasions which is very quick to make.

Preparation time: 10 minutes
Cooking time: 10 to 15 minutes
To serve: 6

6 veal escalopes
salt
freshly ground black pepper
50 g/2 oz butter
100 g/4 oz button mushrooms, thinly sliced
3 tablespoons Calvados or brandy
150 ml/$\frac{1}{4}$ pint crème fraîche (see page 118) or double cream

Beat the veal escalopes between two sheets of greaseproof paper using a meat mallet or rolling pin until they are very thin. Season well with salt and pepper on both sides. Melt the butter in a deep frying pan and sear the escalopes quickly on both sides. Remove from the pan and keep warm.

Add the mushrooms to the pan and cook for 3 minutes or until soft. Return the veal to the pan and heat through. Warm the Calvados or brandy, set it alight and pour into the frying pan. When the flames have died down, stir in the crème fraîche or cream and adjust the seasoning. Bring just to the boil and serve.

Côtes De Veau A La Comtoise *Veal Chops with Cheese*

FRANCHE-COMTE

The smoked ham of the Franche-Comté has a robust flavour, and together with the local Comté cheese gives the veal in this dish a quite unusual 'bite'.

Preparation time: 5 minutes
Cooking time: 15 minutes
To serve: 6

6 veal chops
salt
freshly ground black pepper
40 g/1$\frac{1}{2}$ oz butter
1 tablespoon oil
6 slices of smoked ham
6 slices of Comté or Gruyère cheese
150 ml/$\frac{1}{4}$ pint white wine

Season the chops well on both sides with salt and pepper. Melt 25 g/1 oz of the butter with the oil in a heavy frying pan and quickly brown the chops on each side. Transfer the chops to a flat ovenproof dish. Lay a piece of ham on top of each one and top with a slice of cheese.

Place under a hot grill or in the top of a hot oven and cook for 5 minutes, or until the cheese has melted, is bubbling and just beginning to brown.

Pour the wine into the frying pan, bring to the boil and allow to bubble for 1 minute, stirring to amalgamate any sediment. Add the remaining butter cut into small pieces to give the sauce a glaze and pour over the chops. Serve very hot.

Côtes de veau à la Comtoise, saucisses aux pommes (page 82) and rognons de porc flambés (page 93)

Blanquette De Veau A L'Ancienne

Veal Stew with Onions, Mushrooms and Cream

SAVOIE

This delicious, comforting dish, like most stews, is probably best made a day or two ahead and left to mature. If this is done, however, the last step – the addition of cream and egg yolks – should be left until the veal is to be reheated and served. The light flavour of the meat is an essential quality, so it is necessary to buy the palest, freshest young veal. The usual accompaniment is noodles or boiled potatoes.

Preparation time: 30 minutes
Cooking time: 2 hours
To serve: 6

1.5 kg/3 lb boneless veal shoulder, cut into 5 cm/2 inch chunks
1 large onion, studded with 2 cloves
2 carrots, quartered
1 celery stick, cut in half
1 leek, cut in half
bouquet garni
salt
freshly ground black pepper
1 litre/1¾ pints fresh chicken stock or canned chicken consommé
18–20 button onions, peeled
50 g/2 oz butter
50 g/2 oz flour
0.5 kg/1 lb small button mushrooms
1 teaspoon lemon juice
3 egg yolks
150 ml/¼ pint single cream
chopped fresh parsley to garnish

Place the veal in a flameproof casserole. Cover with cold water, bring to the boil and blanch for 2 to 3 minutes. Drain and rinse under cold water to remove all traces of scum. Return the veal to the clean casserole.

Place the onion, carrots, celery, leek and bouquet garni on top of the meat. Season and cover with the chicken stock. If any of the meat or vegetables are still exposed, add water. Bring to the boil once again and skim off any scum. Reduce the heat and simmer the veal, partially covered, for 1½ hours or until tender but not overcooked.

Meanwhile, place the small onions in a saucepan, together with some of the stock from the simmering casserole, and bring to the boil. Cover, reduce the heat and simmer for 20 minutes, or until the onions are tender. Remove the onions with a slotted spoon and put aside. Pour the liquid into the simmering veal.

When the veal is tender, pour the contents of the saucepan into a colander over a bowl. Melt the 50 g/2 oz of butter in a saucepan and add the flour. Cook for 2 minutes, stirring continuously. Ladle in 1 litre/1¾ pints of the veal stock, stirring as the sauce thickens. Add the mushrooms and lemon juice and gently fold into the sauce. Cook for about 5 minutes then add the veal and the reserved onions to the sauce and mushrooms.

Beat the egg yolks and cream in a bowl until thoroughly combined. Stir into the veal. Heat again briefly, to thicken the sauce, but do not allow to boil.

Spoon the blanquette into the centre of a heated serving plate and arrange cooked noodles or potatoes around the edge. Garnish with the parsley, and serve.

Cassoulet De Toulouse

Casserole of Beans with Pork and Lamb

LANGUEDOC

Three towns in the Languedoc – Castelnaudry, Toulouse and Carcassone – claim this classic dish as their own. Each has its own particular variation, but the basic ingredients of the cassoulet are haricot beans, a well-flavoured pork sausage, and a piece of preserved goose (*confit d'oie*). The latter can be bought canned, but if it is not available a perfectly good *cassoulet* can be made without it. This version, from Toulouse, which includes lamb as well as pork, is particularly satisfying.

Essential is a really large cassoulet pot, or casserole.

Preparation time: 1 hour
Cooking time: about 3 hours
Oven temperature: 150°C, 300°F, Gas Mark 2
To serve: 10 to 12

1 kg/2 lb dried white haricot beans
225 g/8 oz salt pork or bacon, in one piece
0.5 kg/1 lb loin or shoulder of pork, boned
2 tablespoons oil or fat from preserved goose
2 onions, thinly sliced
3 garlic cloves, finely chopped
1 small shoulder of lamb (or ½ large one), boned
1 piece preserved goose (optional)
0.5 kg/1 lb piece coarse pork and garlic sausage
4 tablespoons concentrated tomato purée
1.75 litres/3 pints water
salt
freshly ground black pepper
1 bouquet garni
100 g/4 oz fresh breadcrumbs (see method)

Rinse the beans in cold water, then put into a large saucepan. Cover with cold water, bring slowly to the boil and simmer for 5 minutes. Remove from the heat, cover and leave to soak in the water while you prepare the remaining ingredients.

Remove the rind from the salt pork or bacon, and from the pork, and cut it into small squares.

Heat the oil or goose fat in a large frying pan and fry the onions and garlic until softened. Add the pieces of rind and fry gently for 5 minutes. Raise the heat and brown on all sides, in turn, the pork and salt pork, the shoulder of lamb, the piece of goose and the sausage. Remove each from the pan when it is browned and set aside. Add the tomato purée to the pan with a little of the water, stir well to amalgamate any sediment and bring quickly to the boil.

Drain the beans, rinse them and put them in a clean saucepan with the remaining cold water. Bring to the boil, then pour the beans and water into the cassoulet pot. Add the contents of the frying pan, salt and pepper to taste and stir well. Bury the salt pork or bacon, the pork, the shoulder of lamb, the preserved goose and the sausage among the beans, add the bouquet garni, and bring to simmering point on top of the stove.

Sprinkle on a thick layer of breadcrumbs and place the cassoulet pot in the oven. Cook for 2 to 3 hours. From time to time press down the crust which will have formed on top and sprinkle on a further layer of breadcrumbs. Tradition has it that the crust must be pressed down and renewed seven times, but after three times you should have a lovely golden crust. Larger pieces of meat should be cut up before serving.

Truffade *Potato, Bacon and Cheese Pancake*

AUVERGNE

This recipe is found with variations all over the area of the *massif central*, using whichever is the local cheese, which might be a Tomme, a Beaufort, a Gruyère or a Cantal. Serve these potato pancakes on their own as a light supper dish, or to accompany a robust meat dish.

Preparation time: 20 minutes
Cooking time: about 15 minutes
To serve: 4

225 g/8 oz cheese (see above), diced
0.5 kg/1 lb potatoes, peeled and sliced wafer-thin
salt
freshly ground black pepper
100 g/4 oz streaky bacon, diced
25 g/1 oz lard

Make in two or four batches, using half or a quarter of the ingredients for each batch.

Mingle the cheese gently with the potatoes and season the mixture with salt and pepper. Melt the bacon in a frying pan over a low heat until the fat begins to run. Add the lard to the frying pan, raise the heat and when the fat begins to smoke, add the potato mixture to the pan. Lower the heat and cook, stirring, for 5 minutes, then leave to cook over a moderate heat until the bottom of the pancake is crisp and brown. Invert onto heated plates to serve.

Ris De Veau A La Crème *Calf's Sweetbreads in Cream*

BRITTANY

Offal is one of the mainstays of French cuisine, and sweetbreads are among the most delicate and prized items of the repertoire. Calf sweetbreads are the best, although lamb sweetbreads can also be used. The soaking, blanching and pressing can be done a day ahead of time, leaving the actual cooking to take no longer than the average supper dish. Some butchers sell their sweetbreads already prepared, so ask when you buy.

These sweetbreads are particularly delicious served in a warm vol-au-vent or pastry case.

Preparation time: 1 hour (plus soaking and pressing)
Cooking time: 45 minutes
Oven temperature: 170°C, 325°F, Gas Mark 3
To serve: 4

2 pairs of calf's sweetbreads
4 long strips of streaky bacon
1 large onion, sliced
2 carrots, sliced
150 ml/¼ pint chicken stock
150 ml/¼ pint white wine
50 g/2 oz butter (optional)
150 ml/¼ pint double cream
2 teaspoons chopped fresh parsley
salt
freshly ground black pepper

If the sweetbreads have not been prepared, soak them in cold water until they turn white. This usually requires about 3 hours, and the water should be changed three or four times to remove impurities. When the sweetbreads are clean, fill a saucepan with cold salted water, add the sweetbreads and bring to the boil, stirring constantly but gently to agitate the sweetbreads and continue the clearing process. When the water begins to boil, remove the sweetbreads and drain them thoroughly. Their consistency is now much tougher, and they can be handled and trimmed.

After trimming, put the sweetbreads on paper towels, on either a board or plate, and cover with a heavy weight. Press the sweetbreads for at least one hour, or overnight.

Wrap each pressed sweetbread with a large piece of streaky bacon. Place the onion and carrots on the bottom of a flameproof casserole. Lay the sweetbreads on top of the vegetables and pour over the stock and wine. Scatter over the parsley. Bring the casserole to the boil gently, then remove from the heat, cover and cook in the oven for about 45 minutes.

When the sweetbreads are tender, remove with a slotted spoon and place on a heated serving dish. Alternatively, they may be browned very gently in the butter over a low heat, while the sauce is being made. Bring the cooking liquid to the boil and boil briskly to reduce by half. Turn down the heat, stir in the cream, parsley and add salt and pepper to taste. Strain the sauce over the sweetbreads, and serve.

Foie de veau à la Lyonnaise and truffade

Foie De Veau A La Lyonnaise *Calf's Liver with Onions*

LYONNAIS

Onions are one of the hallmarks of Lyonnaise cooking, and this is a delicious way of preparing liver.

Preparation time: 15 minutes
Cooking time: 10 minutes
To serve: 4

0.5 kg/1 lb calf's or lamb's liver
1 tablespoon flour
100 g/4 oz butter
0.5 kg/1 lb onions, thinly sliced
salt
freshly ground black pepper
1 tablespoon wine vinegar

Cut the liver into thick slices, diagonally, and dust each slice lightly with flour. Melt half the butter in a frying pan. When it is foaming and just beginning to darken, add the liver and brown quickly on both sides. Remove to a heated serving dish and keep hot.

Add the remaining butter to the frying pan, heat and add the onions. Cook over a high heat until they brown, stirring so that they brown evenly. Season to taste with salt and pepper, then add the vinegar and bring quickly to the boil.

Pile the onion mixture over the liver and serve very hot.

Rognons D'Agneau Au Champagne *Lambs' Kidneys Cooked in Champagne*

CHAMPAGNE

The Champagne that would be used for this delicate and luxurious dish, which can of course also be made with veal kidneys, would be the still Champagne, or *Champagne nature* of the region, which unfortunately can only be drunk locally as it is not thought to export well. Any other good dry white wine may be used instead. Serve with a simple green salad.

Preparation time: 15 minutes
Cooking time: 20 minutes
To serve: 6

100 g/4 oz butter
12 lambs' kidneys, skinned, cored and thickly sliced
6 to 8 shallots, finely chopped
225 g/8 oz mushrooms, thinly sliced
1 tablespoon flour
150 ml/¼ pint still Champagne or white wine
salt
freshly ground black pepper
2 tablespoons crème fraîche (see page 118) or double cream
squeeze of lemon juice

Melt half the butter in a heavy-based frying pan, add the kidneys and cook until they change colour.

Meanwhile melt the remaining butter in a small heavy saucepan and cook the shallots until they are soft and golden. Add the mushrooms, raise the heat and cook quickly for 2 minutes. Remove from the heat and keep warm.

Sprinkle the kidneys with the flour, stir well and cook without browning for 2 minutes. Stir in the wine to make a smooth sauce and incorporate any sediment on the bottom of the pan. Cover and simmer for 5 minutes or until the kidneys are cooked.

Stir in the mushroom and shallot mixture and salt and pepper to taste, then add the cream and lemon juice. Bring quickly to the boil and serve very hot.

Rognons De Veau Au Chablis *Veal Kidneys Cooked in Chablis*

BURGUNDY

The subtle but full flavour of a Chablis wine blends beautifully with the delicate taste and texture of veal kidneys. If these are not available, you can make the dish with lamb's or pig's kidneys, but it will not be quite so delicate. Serve with plain boiled rice.

Preparation time: 20 minutes
Cooking time: 20 minutes
To serve: 4

4 veal kidneys, sliced
1 tablespoon oil
salt
freshly ground black pepper
pinch of dried thyme
1 bay leaf, crumbled
50 g/2 oz butter
1 tablespoon finely chopped shallots
¼ bottle of Chablis
juice of ½ lemon (or less, according to taste)
½ tablespoon finely chopped fresh parsley

Sprinkle the kidneys with the oil, salt and pepper and the herbs and leave for at least 10 minutes.

Melt half the butter in a frying pan, add the kidney slices and fry quickly until they have changed colour. Turn into a heated serving dish and keep hot.

Add the shallots to the pan and sweat until they soften. Add the wine, bring to the boil and boil for a few minutes to reduce, stirring well to loosen any sediment on the bottom of the pan.

Add the lemon juice and salt and pepper to taste, then stir in the remaining butter, cut into small pieces, to give the sauce a glaze. Pour the sauce over the kidneys, sprinkle with the parsley and serve very hot.

Tripe A La Mode De Caen *Tripe in the Caen Manner*

NORMANDY

This famous dish can often be bought cooked and ready to serve in Normandy and large cities in France. It is usually of excellent quality because it is made in large quantities by first class specialists. However, although it's preparation is long, it is easy to make.

Preparation time: 15 minutes
Cooking time: 6 hours
Oven temperature: 150°C, 300°F, Gas Mark 2
Serve: 6

1 kg/2 lb dressed tripe
1–2 cow heels
salt
freshly ground black pepper
2 bay leaves
2 sprigs of parsley
4 large onions, peeled
4 cloves
4 leeks, sliced
2 carrots, sliced
600 ml/1 pint cider or dry white wine
4 tablespoons Calvados (optional)

Wash the tripe very thoroughly and blanch it, then cut into small pieces. Divide up the cow heels. Place in a strong casserole with the tripe, seasoning, herbs, the onions (each with a clove stuck in it) and the sliced leeks and carrots. Add the cider or wine and the Calvados (if used). Cover and cook in the oven for 6 hours.

This dish may be left overnight. Remove the fat from the surface and take out the cow heel bones and the herbs before reheating for serving.

Rognons De Porc Flambés *Kidneys Flambé*

LORRAINE

A very simple, quick and economical dish, this is delicious enough for a special occasion. Serve with rice or noodles, followed by a simple green salad.

Preparation time: 10 minutes
Cooking time: 10 to 15 minutes
To serve: 4

75 g/3 oz butter
8 shallots, finely chopped
4 pigs' kidneys, skinned, cored and sliced
2 tablespoons brandy
pinch of cayenne
pinch of dried thyme
salt
freshly ground black pepper
120 ml/4 fl oz white wine
1 tablespoon finely chopped fresh parsley

Melt 50 g/2 oz of the butter in a heavy frying pan, add the shallots and fry until softened. Add the kidneys and cook over a fairly high heat for 3 minutes, stirring.

When the kidneys have all changed colour, add the brandy and set alight. Take off the heat and wait for the flames to die down.

Add the cayenne, thyme and salt and pepper to taste. Return to a moderate heat and cook for 2 to 3 minutes, until the kidneys are cooked. Add the wine, stir well to amalgamate, bring to the boil and let the sauce bubble for 2 minutes. Add the remaining butter, cut into small pieces, to give the sauce a glaze. Sprinkle with the parsley and serve very hot.

Lièvre Angoumois

Hare in Wine and Currant Jelly
GUYENNE

This dish is named after the town and region of Angouleme, a rich area bounded on the left by the cognac distilleries of the Charente and on the right by the truffles and walnuts of the Perigord. It is fairly hilly country, abundant with all kinds of game. Numerous soft fruits – including currants, grapes and cherries – are commercial products of the Angoumois, and this recipe combines the cultivated bounty with that of the wild.

Preparation time: 15 minutes
Cooking time: 4 hours
Oven temperature: 170°C, 325°F, Gas Mark 3
To serve: 6

1 hare, skinned and jointed
25 g/1 oz lard
50 g/2 oz bacon, chopped
1 onion, stuck with 2 cloves
1 carrot, sliced
1 stick celery, sliced
1 litre/$1\frac{3}{4}$ pints beef stock
bouquet garni
juice of $\frac{1}{2}$ lemon
3 tablespoons flour
1 teaspoon redcurrant jelly
1 wine glass red wine

Place the pieces of the hare in a large flameproof casserole, together with the lard and bacon. Sauté the hare over a medium heat for about 5 minutes or until lightly browned. Add the vegetables and enough stock to cover the hare. Add the bouquet garni and lemon juice. Bring to the boil, then cover and cook in the oven for 4 hours, checking occasionally to make sure that there is enough liquid in the pot. Remove the onion.

Just before serving, skim any fat from the casserole. Blend the flour with a little cold water until smooth, then stir slowly into the casserole. Add the jelly and wine and simmer, uncovered, for a few minutes until the sauce has reduced and thickened.

Râble De Lièvre A La Crème

LORRAINE

This method of cooking hare, which shows the influence of German cuisine in this region, mellows the strong flavour of the hare, and makes it into a rich and velvety delicacy.

Preparation time: 15 minutes (plus 3 hours minimum marinating)
Cooking time: 50 minutes
Oven temperature: 190°C, 375°F, Gas Mark 5
To serve: 4 to 6

1 saddle of hare, including the hind legs, skinned
1 tablespoon oil
1 teaspoon wine vinegar
salt
freshly ground black pepper
1 thyme branch
1 rosemary branch
50 g/2 oz butter
150 ml/$\frac{1}{4}$ pint crème fraîche (see page 118) or double cream

Faisan à la vigneronne (page 60), rable de lièvre à la piron and lapin à la moutarde (page 96)

Saddle of Hare with Cream

Lay the hare in a roasting pan, dribble on the oil and the vinegar, sprinkle with salt and pepper and lay the thyme and rosemary on top. Leave to marinate for several hours, turning the hare over occasionally.

When ready to cook, remove thyme and rosemary, melt the butter and when sizzling, pour over the hare. Place in the oven and cook for 40 minutes, basting and turning the hare over several times. Take great care not to let the sediment at the bottom of the pan burn, as this will give a very bitter taste; if necessary add a little more oil.

Remove the hare – the meat should be just pink inside – carve into thick slices and keep warm on a heated serving dish.

Add the cream to the juices in the roasting pan and bring quickly to the boil, scraping up any sediment on the bottom of the pan. Boil until the sauce thickens. Season to taste with salt and pepper, adding a few drops more wine vinegar if necessary, and serve very hot.

Râble De Lièvre A La Piron

Marinated Saddle of Hare with Grapes
BURGUNDY

This is one of the great classics of Burgundian cooking, traditionally eaten to celebrate the end of the grape harvest. Extravagant though it is, it is a beautiful dish, well worth making for a special occasion.

Preparation time: 30 minutes plus 2 to 3 days marinating
Cooking time: 25 to 30 minutes
Oven temperature: 190°C, 375°F, Gas Mark 5
To serve: 4 to 6

100 g/4 oz pork or bacon fat, cut into larding strips
1 saddle of hare
4 shallots, roughly chopped
1 garlic clove, roughly chopped
1 fresh thyme branch
2 bay leaves, crumbled
1 celery stick, roughly chopped
salt
freshly ground black pepper
200 ml/$\frac{1}{3}$ pint eau-de-vie de marc
100 g/4 oz butter, melted
1 tablespoon wine vinegar
2 tablespoons double cream
100 g/4 oz white grapes, peeled and seeded
100 g/4 oz black grapes, peeled and seeded

Thread the pork or bacon at strips into the flesh of the hare at intervals, using a larding needle. Put into a bowl, add the shallots, garlic, herbs, celery and salt and pepper and pour over 150 ml/$\frac{1}{4}$ pint of the eau-de-vie de marc. Leave in a cool place to marinate for 2 or 3 days, turning the hare frequently.

Drain the hare, reserving the marinade, and place in a roasting pan. Sprinkle with a little more salt and pepper, pour on the melted butter and roast in the oven until just cooked – the inside must remain pink.

Remove the hare to a heated serving dish. Warm the remaining marc, pour over the hare and set alight. Leave until the flames die down.

Pour the strained marinade into the roasting pan, add the vinegar and bring quickly to the boil. Add the cream and stir until smooth. Adjust the seasoning. Pour the sauce over the hare, surround with the grapes and serve.

Lapin A La Moutarde *Rabbit Cooked with Mustard*

BURGUNDY

Stuffed, and covered with the local Dijon mustard, this rabbit dish is a highly tasty speciality of the area.

Preparation time: 30 minutes
Cooking time: about 1 hour
Oven temperature: 190°C, 375°F, Gas Mark 5
To serve: 4 to 6

1 rabbit, skinned and prepared
1 tablespoon brandy
50 g/2 oz butter
1 onion, finely chopped
4 shallots, finely chopped
2 garlic cloves, finely chopped
1 rabbit liver, finely chopped
100 g/4 oz chicken livers, finely chopped
100 g/4 oz stale white bread
150 ml/¼ pint milk
½ tablespoon finely chopped fresh parsley
½ teaspoon dried thyme
1 bay leaf, crumbled
salt
freshly ground black pepper
1 egg, beaten
3 tablespoons Dijon mustard
2 tablespoons fine dry white breadcrumbs
150 ml/¼ pint crème fraîche (see page 118)

Rub the rabbit inside and out with the brandy.

Melt half the butter in a frying pan, add the onion, shallots and garlic and fry until softened. Take the pan off the heat and gently mix in the chopped rabbit and chicken livers.

Soak the bread briefly in the milk, squeeze out and place in a mixing bowl. Add the onion and liver mixture, the parsley, thyme and bay leaf, season generously with salt and pepper and bind together with the egg. Stuff the rabbit with this mixture and place in a roasting pan.

Spread the mustard all over the rabbit and sprinkle with the breadcrumbs, patting them in firmly. Dot with the remaining butter and roast in the oven, basting from time to time and adding a little more butter if necessary. When the rabbit is cooked, remove it to a heated serving platter. Keep hot.

Add the cream to the juices in the roasting pan, stir well and add a little water if necessary to remove all the sediment from the bottom of the pan. Bring quickly to the boil, adjust the seasoning and pour over the rabbit before serving.

Côtelettes De Chevreuil d'Uzes *Venison Chops Uzes Style*

LANGUEDOC

Chevreuil is the young roebuck of the area, which is very tender and can take quick cooking. Older meat may need marinating overnight in a mixture of olive oil and white wine.

Preparation time: 10 minutes
Cooking time: 20 minutes
Serves: 4

4 venison chops
2 tablespoons oil
50 g/2 oz butter
4 slices of bread, cut into heart shapes
5 tablespoons wine vinegar
225 ml/8 fl oz stock
300 ml/½ pint single cream
1 orange, the rind cut into thin strips and a little juice
2 tablespoons blanched almonds
4 small gherkins, cut into thin strips
freshly ground black pepper

Sauté the chops on both sides in the oil. Arrange them in a warm serving dish in the shape of an overlapping circle and keep warm. Add the butter to the pan in which the chops were cooked and fry the bread. Arrange the croûtons alternately with the chops. Scrape the bottom of the pan and stir in the vinegar to lift the sediment. Add the stock and cream. Bring to the boil and reduce to thicken slightly.

Pass the sauce through a sieve and return to a clean pan. Add the strips of orange rind, a little juice, the almonds, gherkins and season with black pepper. Reheat the sauce and pour over the chops to serve.

Vegetables

Gratin Dauphinois *Gratiné Potatoes Baked in Cream*

DAUPHINE

An utterly creamy, melting-in-the-mouth potato dish, which is good enough to be eaten on its own but also enhances dishes of chicken or veal or baked fish.

Preparation time: 30 minutes
Cooking time: 2 hours
Oven temperature: 190°C, 375°F, Gas Mark 5
To serve: 4 to 6

1 kg/2 lb potatoes, peeled and very thinly sliced
1 garlic clove, halved
50 g/2 oz butter
salt
freshly ground black pepper
450 ml/¾ pint double cream

Soak the potatoes in cold water for at least 10 minutes to extract some of the starch, then drain and pat them dry.

Rub a large shallow ovenproof gratin dish with the cut surface of the clove of garlic, then butter it generously, using 15 g/½ oz of the butter. Arrange a layer of potato slices in the bottom of the dish, sprinkle with salt and pepper, and dot with small pieces of butter. Continue until all the potatoes have been used.

Bring the cream just to the boil in a saucepan. Pour over the potatoes and dot with the remaining butter. Bake in the oven until the potatoes have absorbed all the cream and are very tender. If the potatoes seem to be drying out too quickly, cover with a sheet of greaseproof or wax paper or foil.

When ready, the top should be golden brown. Raise the heat and place the dish on the top oven shelf towards the end if necessary.

Gratin Savoyard *Gratiné Potatoes*

SAVOIE

This is the simplest of the potato gratins, which are among the best loved specialities of this moutainous, central district of France. It makes a particularly good accompaniment to beef or game.

Preparation time: 30 minutes
Cooking time: 1 to 1½ hours
Oven temperature: 200°C, 400°F, Gas Mark 6
To serve: 4 to 6

1 kg/2 lb potatoes, peeled and very thinly sliced
2 garlic cloves, 1 halved and 1 very finely chopped
50 g/2 oz butter
salt
freshly ground black pepper
100 g/4 oz Gruyère or Comté cheese, grated
300 ml/½ pint boiling stock

Soak the potatoes in cold water for at least 10 minutes to extract some of the starch, then drain and pat them dry.

Rub a large shallow ovenproof gratin dish with the cut surface of the halved clove of garlic, then butter the dish very generously, using nearly half the butter. Arrange a layer of potato slices on the bottom of the dish and sprinkle with salt and pepper, a little chopped garlic and some grated cheese. Repeat until all the potatoes have been used, but keep aside a good 2 tablespoons of the cheese. Pour on the hot stock.

Finish with a thick sprinkling of cheese and dot with the remaining butter. Cook in the oven until the potatoes have absorbed all the liquid and are tender, and the top is golden brown and crisp.

If the potatoes are cooked but the top not browned, raise the oven heat and place the dish very near the top of the oven for the last 10 minutes, or brown under the grill.

Gratin Dauphinoise and gratin Savoyarde

Carottes Vichy *Cooked Carrots*

BOURBONNAIS

Carrots are used a great deal in the cooking of this part of central France. Vichy water, which is particularly soft, may be used locally, but ordinary tap water will also do perfectly well for this way of cooking carrots. It is one of the simplest and best in bringing out their flavour.
Young carrots may be left whole; older ones should be cut into thick rings.

Preparation time: 10 minutes
Cooking time: 15 to 20 minutes
To serve: 4

0.5 kg/1 lb carrots, whole or sliced (see above)
150 ml/¼ pint water
25 g/1 oz butter
1 sugar lump
salt
freshly ground black pepper
1 tablespoon finely chopped fresh parsley

Put the carrots into a heavy saucepan with the water, half the butter, the sugar and salt and pepper and simmer until the carrots are just tender and all the water has evaporated. Watch that they do not boil dry and add a little more water if necessary.

Add the remaining butter and swirl around the pan to melt it and coat the carrots. Sprinkle with the parsley before serving.

Carottes A La Nivernaise *Glazed Carrots and Onions*

NIVERNAIS

One of the classic ways of garnishing a meat dish, these glazed carrots and small onions are equally delicious with beef, veal or lamb, or eaten alone as a vegetable side dish. Use small young carrots whole; cut older ones into thick slices. Use small silverskin or pickling onions, or, if possible, the small flat French onions.

Preparation time: 20 minutes
Cooking time: 20 to 30 minutes
To serve: 4 to 6

225 g/8 oz carrots, whole or thickly sliced (see above)
225 g/8 oz small onions, peeled
scant 300 ml/$\frac{1}{2}$ pint water
25 g/1 oz butter
1 sugar lump
salt
freshly ground black pepper
2 tablespoons meat stock or juice from a roasted joint
1 teaspoon sugar

Put the carrots and onions into a heavy saucepan with the water, half the butter, the sugar lump and salt and pepper and simmer until all the water has evaporated and the vegetables are just tender.

Add the meat stock, sugar and the remaining butter, raise the heat a little and cook until just beginning to brown slightly.

Adjust the seasoning before serving.

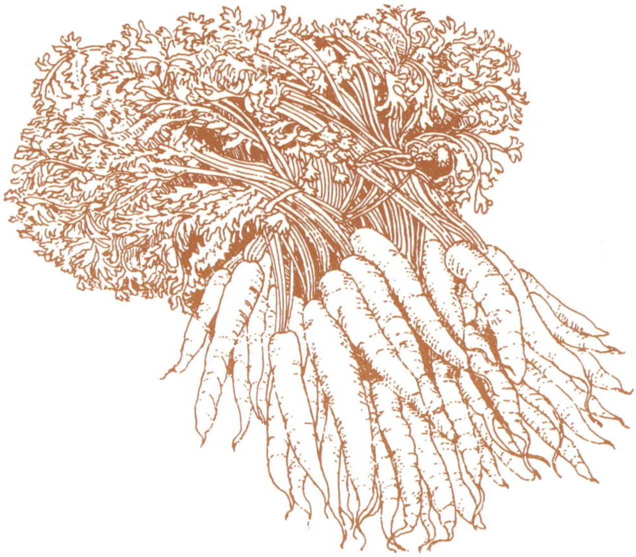

Petits Pois A La Nivernaise *Peas with Carrots and Onions*

NIVERNAIS

A delicious and very pretty mixture of fresh young vegetables, this should really be eaten on its own, after the main dish.

Preparation time: 30 minutes
Cooking time: 30 minutes
To serve: 6

50 g/2 oz butter
2 bunches of young carrots, scrubbed or scraped
225 g/8 oz silverskin or pickling onions, peeled
1 small lettuce, leaves separated
0.5 kg/1 lb shelled peas
salt
freshly ground black pepper
pinch of sugar
150 ml/$\frac{1}{4}$ pint water
2 tablespoons crème fraîche (see page 118) or double cream

Melt the butter in a large, heavy saucepan, add the carrots, onions and lettuce leaves and turn well so that they become evenly coated with butter. Cover and sweat very gently for 5 minutes.

Add the peas, salt and pepper, the sugar and water, cover again and simmer gently until the peas are just tender. All the vegetables should be cooked through, but not too soft.

Stir in the cream, adjust the seasoning and serve with the cooking liquid.

Les Navets Au Sucre *Turnips with Sugar*

MAINE

Root vegetables grow well in this northern part of France, and are eaten a great deal, especially in the country. They are always eaten young, and usually served on their own, so that their full flavour, brought out in the cooking, can be properly appreciated.

Preparation time: 10 minutes
Cooking time: 15 to 25 minutes
To serve: 4

25 g/1 oz butter
25 g/1 oz sugar
0.5 kg/1 lb young turnips, peeled
4 tablespoons water or stock
salt
freshly ground black pepper
1 tablespoon finely chopped fresh parsley

Melt the butter and sugar together in a saucepan over a low heat. Add the whole turnips and cook gently for 5 minutes, turning them so that they become evenly coated with the butter and sugar. Add the water or stock and salt and pepper to taste, then cover and simmer until the turnips are tender, shaking the pan from time to time.

Adjust the seasoning and sprinkle with the parsley before serving.

Marrons Braisés *Braised Chestnuts*

GUYENNE

Inland, throughout the southwestern corner of France, the roads are lined with chestnut trees. Chestnuts are used not only to make the famous marrons glacés and other sweet dishes, but also in savoury cooking, to accompany meat dishes, especially game, or to add body to stuffings or to other vegetables.

Braised as here they make an excellent accompaniment to turkey, venison or other game, and they are also sometimes eaten quite plain in the Limousin, boiled and peeled, with salt, pepper and a little butter. The easiest way to peel chestnuts is to put them into a large saucepan, cover with cold water, bring to the boil and boil for 2 minutes. Take them out a few at a time, keeping the others hot, and peel as soon as they are cool enough to handle. If towards the end the chestnuts become difficult to peel, bring briefly to the boil again.

Preparation time: 2 minutes (plus peeling chestnuts)
Cooking time: 40 to 50 minutes
To serve: 4 to 6

0.5 kg/1 lb chestnuts, peeled
25 g/1 oz butter
300 ml/½ pint stock
salt
freshly ground black pepper

Put all the ingredients into a heavy saucepan, cover and bring to the boil. Simmer for 40 to 50 minutes or until the chestnuts are tender without having disintegrated, and all the liquid has been absorbed. If necessary, leave the lid off the pan for the last 15 minutes cooking, to allow excess moisture to evaporate.

Adjust the seasoning before serving.

Pipérade *Ragoût of Peppers and Tomatoes*

LANGUEDOC

A simple dish, from the Basque country, this can be served as an appetizer or as a light main dish.

Preparation time: 15 minutes
Cooking time: 30 minutes
To serve: 4 to 6

2 tablespoons olive oil or goose or pork dripping
2 large onions, thinly sliced
1 garlic clove, finely chopped (optional)
0.5 kg/1 lb peppers, cored, seeded and cut into strips
0.5 kg/1 lb tomatoes, skinned and roughly chopped
6 eggs
1 teaspoon finely chopped fresh parsley or basil
salt
freshly ground black pepper
triangles of fried bread to garnish

Heat the oil or dripping in a deep frying pan or shallow flameproof casserole, add the onions and garlic and fry gently until golden yellow. Add the peppers and cook for 10 to 15 minutes, or until they are soft. Stir in the tomatoes, raise the heat a little and cook until most of the moisture has evaporated and the tomatoes have reduced to a thick pulp.

Beat the eggs together with the herbs and salt and pepper to taste and pour into the pan. Stir gently until they begin to set. Remove the pan from the heat while the mixture is still creamy. Serve garnished with the bread triangles.

Pipérade, aillade de Toulouse (page 112), courgettes aux fines herbes (page 104) and pissaladière (page 104).

Petits Pois A La Française Peas Cooked with Lettuce

NIVERNAIS

Tender young peas are a joy, and should be eaten, as they usually are in France, all alone, with their cooking juice, so that their full flavour is appreciated. This recipe can only be made in spring and early summer, when all the vegetables are young and fresh.

Preparation time: 10 minutes
Cooking time: 15 to 25 minutes
To serve: 4 to 6

50 g/2 oz butter
5 to 6 spring onions, sliced
2 lettuce hearts, shredded
salt
freshly ground black pepper
1.5 kg/3 lb fresh young peas, shelled
1 teaspoon sugar
150 ml/¼ pint chicken stock or water

Melt the butter in a heavy saucepan, add the spring onions and allow them to soften. Add half the lettuce hearts and salt and pepper to taste, then stir in the peas. Sprinkle with the sugar and cover with the remaining shredded lettuce.

Pour in the stock or water and bring to the boil. Cover tightly and simmer for 10 to 20 minutes, or until the peas are just tender. Serve hot, with all the juice.

Haricots De Soissons A La Crème Haricot Beans in Cream Sauce

ILE DE FRANCE

The beans from Soissons are the aristocrats of haricot beans. Small and pointed, with a slight green tinge, they are not only very pretty, but also have a special flavour. They are scarce and therefore expensive, but if you do find them, they will be fresh and should not need long soaking or cooking. They are much too good not to be eaten as a special side dish on their own.

Preparation time: 15 minutes plus soaking time
Cooking time: about 1 hour
To serve: 6

0.5 kg/1 lb dried Soissons haricot beans, soaked in cold water for 4 to 5 hours
1 bouquet garni
25 g/1 oz butter
1 small onion, finely chopped
100 g/4 oz smoked pork or bacon, finely diced
150 ml/¼ pint double cream or crème fraîche (see page 118)
salt
freshly ground black pepper
1 tablespoon chopped fresh parsley

Drain the beans and put them into a saucepan with enough fresh cold water to cover. Add the bouquet garni, bring to the boil and simmer gently for at least 45 minutes until the beans are tender but have not lost their shape. Drain and keep warm.

Melt the butter in a heavy saucepan, add the onion and smoked pork or bacon and cook until the onion is soft. Add the beans and turn well to mix with the onion and pork. Stir in the cream and bring just to the boil. Simmer until the cream has thickened a little.

Add salt and pepper to taste and sprinkle with parsley before serving.

Pissaladière *Onion, Anchovy and Olive Tart*

PROVENCE

The pungent Provençal first cousin to the Italian Pizza, serve *pissaladière* as an appetizer, or as a light luncheon dish, accompanied by a salad.

Preparation time: 40 minutes plus 1 hour rising
Cooking time: 50 minutes
Oven temperature: 200°C, 400°F, Gas Mark 6; reduced to 190°C, 375°F, Gas Mark 5
To serve: 6

Dough
15 g/½ oz fresh yeast
2 tablespoons lukewarm water
150 g/5 oz plain flour
salt
1 egg, beaten
1 tablespoon olive oil

Filling
4 tablespoons olive oil
0.5 kg/1¼ lb onions, thinly sliced
salt
freshly ground black pepper
1 × 50 g/1¾ oz can anchovy fillets, drained and halved
50 g/2 oz black olives, stoned

Dissolve the yeast in the water and leave in a warm place until frothy. Sift the flour and salt into a warmed bowl, and make a well in the centre. Add the yeast mixture, egg and olive oil and mix together with a wooden spoon. Knead the dough until it is springy and comes away clean from the sides of the bowl. Leave in a warm place to rise for about 1 hour, or until it has doubled in bulk. Meanwhile, heat the olive oil in a heavy frying pan, add the onions and fry gently until they are quite soft and yellow. Do not allow them to brown. Season to taste with salt and pepper.

When the dough has risen, knead again, form into a ball and place on a well-oiled 30 cm/12 inch round baking tin. Gently press the dough from the centre outwards until the baking tin is evenly covered. Spread on the onions, then make a criss-cross pattern on top with the halved anchovy fillets and intersperse with the olives. Leave to rise again for 15 minutes, then place in the centre of the oven. Bake for 40 to 50 minutes, turning down the oven temperature for the last 15 minutes if the crust is turning too dark.

Cut into pieces before serving.

Courgettes Aux Fines Herbes *Courgettes with Herbs*

PROVENCE

This dish from Provence is made with fresh herbs, which bring out the delicate flavour of the courgettes.

Preparation time: 10 minutes (plus 1 hour draining)
Cooking time: 10 to 15 minutes
To serve: 4 to 6

1 kg/2 lb courgettes, coarsely grated
salt
3 tablespoons olive oil
large squeeze of lemon juice
1 tablespoon finely chopped fresh basil and parsley
freshly ground black pepper

Spread out the courgettes on a clean towel. Sprinkle with salt, then leave to drain in the towel in a colander for 1 hour. Squeeze out all the moisture through the towel.

Heat the oil in a frying pan, add the courgettes and cook over a medium heat until they are tender, stirring from time to time. Sprinkle with lemon juice and herbs, season to taste with salt and pepper and toss gently before serving.

Ratatouille *Provençal Vegetable Ragoût*

PROVENCE

A speciality of Provence, ratatouille can be found, with local variations, all around the Mediterranean coast. It can be eaten hot or cold, on its own as an hors d'oeuvre or as a vegetable side dish, and goes equally well with fish or meat.

Preparation time: 30 minutes (plus 1 hour draining the vegetables)
Cooking time: 1 hour
To serve: 6 to 8

0.5 kg/1 lb aubergines, sliced
0.5 kg/1 lb courgettes, sliced
salt
150 ml/$\frac{1}{4}$ pint olive oil
3 large onions, sliced
2 garlic cloves, finely chopped
3 peppers (1 red, 1 yellow and 1 green, if possible), cored, seeded and cut into strips
0.5 kg/1 lb tomatoes, skinned and seeded
salt
freshly ground black pepper
$\frac{1}{2}$ teaspoon sugar
2 tablespoons finely chopped fresh parsley or basil and parsley

Sprinkle the aubergines and the courgettes liberally with salt and leave in separate colanders to drain for 1 hour. When they are ready, rinse, squeeze out excess moisture and pat dry.

Heat the oil in a flameproof casserole, add the onions and garlic and fry until softened. Add the aubergines and cook, stirring well, until they become soft and yellow.

Add the courgettes and peppers, cover and cook gently for 30 minutes. Stir in the tomatoes, seasoning and sugar, and cook, uncovered, for a further 30 minutes. The vegetables should be soft and well mixed but retain their shapes, and most of the liquid should be evaporated. Stir in the parsley and basil before serving.

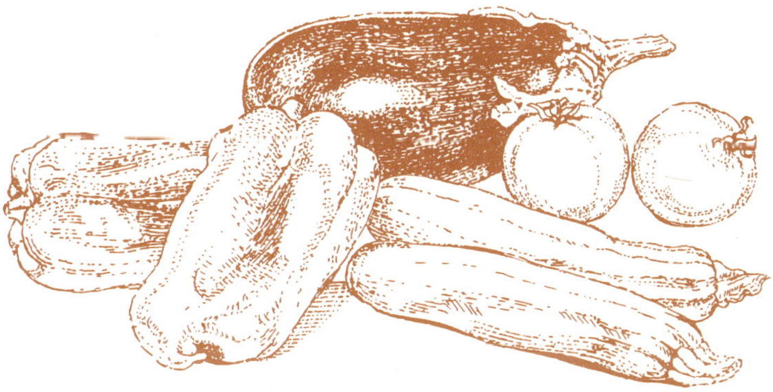

Haricots Verts A La Lyonnaise *French Beans with Onions*

LYONNAISE

The designation 'Lyonnaise' usually means that the recipe is prepared with onions, and this tangy preparation of green beans is no exception. The vinegar gives that extra fillip of flavour.

Preparation time: 10 minutes
Cooking time: 20 minutes
To serve: 4

0.5 kg/1 lb small French stringless beans
salt
75 g/3 oz butter
175 g/6 oz onions, finely sliced
freshly ground black pepper
2 teaspoons vinegar
chopped fresh parsley

Wash the beans and place in a saucepan of boiling salted water. Bring to the boil, then simmer for 10 minutes. Drain the beans thoroughly and dry them with paper towels.

Melt the butter in a pan, add the onions and cook until golden. Add the dry beans and cook over a low heat until the beans have browned slightly. Add salt and pepper to taste, then the vinegar. Toss the ingredients together and transfer to a heated serving dish. Sprinkle with the parsley.

Salade De Lentilles *Lentil Salad*

LANGUEDOC

Made with the little green lentils of Puy, this is an excellent winter salad. Use the new season's lentils only, and they will not need very long to soak or cook.

Preparation time: 10 minutes (plus soaking)
Cooking time: 45 minutes to $1\frac{1}{4}$ hours
To serve: 6

225 g/8 oz lentils, soaked in cold water for a few hours and drained
1 large onion, peeled
2 cloves
1 carrot, peeled
1 bouquet garni
150 ml/$\frac{1}{4}$ pint sauce vinaigrette (see page 110)
100 g/4 oz cervelat or salami-type sausage, diced
1 large onion, or 1 bunch of spring onions, finely chopped
1 garlic clove, finely chopped
1 tablespoon finely chopped fresh parsley

Put the lentils into a large saucepan with the onion stuck with the cloves, the carrot and bouquet garni. Cover with plenty of cold water, bring to the boil and simmer until just tender. Drain well, remove the onion, carrot and bouquet garni and tip the lentils into a salad bowl. Pour over the sauce vinaigrette and stir well. Leave to cool.

Stir in the sausage, chopped onion and garlic and sprinkle with the parsley before serving.

Les Lentilles De Puy Au Petit Salé *Lentils with Salt Pork*

LANGUEDOC

The little grey-green and slate coloured lentils of Puy, in the northern part of the Languedoc, are well known for their flavour. They turn brown when cooked, but keep their shape well, and are excellent for simple winter dishes such as this one, which can be served on its own or as an appetizer or side dish.
The fresher the lentils are, the less soaking or cooking time they will need.

Preparation time: 10 minutes (plus soaking)
Cooking time: 45 minutes to $1\frac{1}{2}$ hours
To serve: 6

25 g/1 oz butter
1 onion, finely chopped
1 garlic clove, finely chopped
225 g/8 oz piece of salt pork, soaked in cold water for a few hours, drained and diced
225 g/8 oz lentils, soaked in cold water for a few hours or overnight and drained
1 bouquet garni
salt
freshly ground black pepper
squeeze of lemon juice
1 tablespoon finely chopped fresh parsley

Melt the butter in a large heavy saucepan, add the onion and garlic and fry until softened. Add the diced pork and turn well. Stir in the lentils. Cover with plenty of cold water, add the bouquet garni and bring to the boil. Simmer until the lentils are tender.

Drain off the liquid and remove the bouquet garni. Adjust the seasoning, add the lemon juice, sprinkle with the parsley and serve hot.

Salade de lentils

Cèpes A La Bordelaise *Mushrooms Cooked in Oil with Shallots and Garlic*

GUYENNE

The area around Bordeaux is particularly rich in mushrooms and especially the wonderfully-flavoured cèpes. If these are not available, cultivated or field mushrooms will also be very good cooked in this way. Serve as a garnish or on croûtes of fried bread as a first course.

Preparation time: 10 minutes
Cooking time: 10 to 12 minutes
To serve: 2 to 3

2 tablespoons olive oil
0.5 kg/1 lb cèpes or other mushrooms, sliced
salt
freshly ground black pepper
good squeeze of lemon juice
2 tablespoons finely chopped shallots
2 garlic cloves, finely chopped
2 tablespoons finely chopped fresh parsley

Heat the oil in a small frying pan and add the cèpes. Cook over a moderate heat, stirring, until they soften. Raise the heat a little to evaporate any excess juice. Season to taste with salt and pepper and add the lemon juice.

Mix the shallots, garlic and parsley together and sprinkle over the ceps in the pan. Do not stir, but allow to cook gently for 2 to 3 minutes. Serve hot.

Chou Rouge A La Limousine *Braised Red Cabbage with Chestnuts*

MARCHE AND LIMOUSINE

This classic red cabbage dish goes particularly well with the game and duck which are plentiful in the region. When poultry and meat dishes are served with a garnish of red cabbage, they are also described as *à la Limousine.*

Preparation time: 15 minutes
Cooking time: 3½ hours
Oven temperature: 170°C, 325°F, Gas Mark 3
To serve: 10

100 g/4 oz streaky bacon, diced
100 g/4 oz onions, finely chopped
1.5 kg/3 lb red cabbage, finely sliced
3 wine glasses red wine
300 ml/½ pint beef stock or consommé
3 tablespoons wine vinegar
3 large bay leaves
5 cloves
large pinch of nutmeg
1 teaspoon salt
freshly ground black pepper
225 g/8 oz dried chestnuts or *1 large can of whole chestnuts in water, drained*

If you are using dried chestnuts, soak in water overnight. Drain and use as directed below.

In a heavy flameproof casserole, cook the bacon over medium heat, stirring frequently, until all the fat has run out and the bacon is light brown. Remove the bacon with a slotted spoon and set aside. Cook the onions in the fat, stirring frequently, until soft and golden. Add the cabbage, gradually, stirring after each addition, to coat with the fat and onions. Cover the casserole tightly and cook over a low heat for 10 minutes.

Add the wine, stock, vinegar, bay leaves, cloves, nutmeg, salt, pepper and the reserved bacon to the cabbage. Cover again and cook in the centre of the oven for 2 hours, checking occasionally to make sure that there is sufficient liquid to keep the cabbage from burning. Add the chestnuts and cook for a further 1 hour. The juice should have reduced to a minimum; if it has not, remove the lid and cook slightly longer until it does. Adjust the seasoning and serve. The dish is even better if it is cooked a day or two ahead of time and reheated when it is needed.

Sauces, Pastry and Fondues

Sauce Vinaigrette *French Salad Dressing*

The most classic and simple of all the salad dressings, this should be freshly made each time, using only the best ingredients. These will vary, however, from one area of France to another: in Normandy or Brittany a cider vinegar might be used instead of a wine one; in the south, pure olive oil is more likely to be used than a corn or nut oil or a combination of oils. The addition of garlic is optional, and becomes stronger the further south you go.

This sauce is frequently served separately, with salads or cold, cooked vegetables. A green lettuce salad, however, is usually dressed just before serving, and well tossed so that every leaf is thinly coated with the dressing.

Preparation time: about 3 minutes
Makes: about 120 ml/4 fl oz

½ garlic clove (optional)
½ teaspoon salt
freshly ground black pepper
¼ teaspoon sugar
½ teaspoon French mustard (optional)
2 tablespoons wine vinegar
6 tablespoons oil

Crush the garlic with the salt and mix in the pepper, sugar and mustard to make a smooth paste. Stir in the vinegar, then slowly add the oil, stirring all the time to amalgamate and make a smooth thick sauce.

Adjust the seasoning before serving.

Sauce Mousseline *Butter, Egg Yolk and Cream Sauce*

Even richer, yet lighter than a sauce hollandaise, this makes a real feast of a simple dish of asparagus.

Preparation time: 15 minutes
Cooking time: 15 to 20 minutes
To serve: 6

3 egg yolks
1 tablespoon lemon juice
1 tablespoon cold water
175 g/6 oz unsalted butter, cut into small cubes
150 ml/¼ pint crème fraîche *(see page 118)*
salt
white pepper

Make an hollandaise sauce (as on page 113). Just before serving, whip the crème fraiche lightly until it just begins to thicken, and fold into the finished hollandaise.

Season to taste with salt and pepper before serving.

Sauce mousseline and sauce vinagrette

Beurre de Montpellier *Montpellier Butter*

LANGUEDOC

A lovely accompaniment to any poached or grilled fish, Montpelier butter is also good on chops or steaks, and for stuffed eggs.

Preparation time: 15 minutes
To serve: 6 to 8

100 g/4 oz fresh spinach, or 50 g/2 oz frozen spinach
bunch of watercress
small bunch of fresh parsley
2 sprigs of fresh tarragon
2 tablespoons capers
6 anchovy fillets
3 hard-boiled egg yolks
100 g/4 oz butter
1 tablespoon olive oil
good squeeze of lemon juice
freshly ground black pepper (optional)

Blanch the spinach, watercress and herbs together in boiling water for 1 minute. If you are using frozen spinach, you need only thaw it. Drain well, squeezing out as much moisture as possible, then put in a mortar or blender with the capers, anchovies and egg yolks. Pound or blend to a fine paste. If you are using a mortar, you may need to push the mixture through a nylon sieve.

Blend in the butter and then the oil, drop by drop, as for making mayonnaise. Add the lemon juice and test for seasoning. This is very unlikely to need salt, but may be improved by a little freshly ground black pepper.

Beurre Blanc *White Butter Sauce*

MAINE

This rich and velvety sauce of delicately flavoured butter is also known as Beurre Nantais, and is traditionally served with pike or trout in the Loire country. It is equally popular in Brittany, where it is served just as frequently with steamed or grilled sea fish.

Preparation time: 15 minutes
Cooking time: 20 minutes
To serve: 6

5 tablespoons white wine
5 tablespoons wine vinegar
1 tablespoon finely chopped shallots
350 g/12 oz butter, at room temperature
salt
freshly ground black pepper
squeeze of lemon juice

Put the wine and vinegar in a small heavy saucepan with the shallots and boil until reduced to about 1 tablespoon. Remove from the heat.

Cut the butter into very small pieces (at least 20) and begin to add these one by one to the pan, beating with a wire whisk or rotary beater. Add each piece of butter only when the previous one has been completely absorbed and return the pan to a very gentle heat after the first few pieces of butter have been incorporated. Remove from the heat as soon as all the butter has been added, and stir in salt and pepper to taste and the lemon juice. Serve warm.

If the sauce is not to be served immediately, place it in a bowl over a pan of warm, not hot, water to keep it at just the right temperature – if it becomes too cold, it will congeal; if too hot, it will separate.

Aillade De Toulouse *Walnut and Garlic Sauce*

LANGUEDOC

A rich, thick liaison of walnuts, garlic and oil, this is sometimes eaten just with some bread dipped in or with crisp vegetables as an hors d'oeuvre, but it is also served as a sauce with cold meat, poultry or ham.

Preparation time: 10 to 15 minutes
To serve: 6

100 g/4 oz walnuts
2 large garlic cloves
salt
freshly ground black pepper
about 5 tablespoons olive oil
squeeze of lemon juice (optional)

Pound, grind or blend the walnuts together with the garlic to form a smooth paste. Season to taste with salt and pepper.

Add the oil drop by drop, stirring or blending continuously as for making mayonnaise, until you have a smooth thick sauce. Adjust the seasoning and add a little lemon juice to taste, if liked.

Sauce Hollandaise *Butter and Egg Yolk Sauce*

This rich but light sauce is delicious with fish, or with such delicate vegetables as asparagus, artichokes or broccoli. It is also excellent served with eggs: the legendary *oeufs benedictine* is merely a poached egg lying on a buttered round of toast or cooked pastry, with a slice on ham on top, and coated with a sauce hollandaise. It is really not difficult to make, provided you give yourself fully to the task.

Preparation time: 10 minutes
Cooking time: 15 to 20 minutes
To serve: 6

3 egg yolks
1 tablespoon lemon juice
1 tablespoon cold water
175 g/6 oz unsalted butter, cut into small cubes
salt
white pepper

Beat the egg yolks with the lemon juice and water in a heatproof bowl until they become quite thick and pale. An electric beater is invaluable for this. Place the bowl over a pan of simmering water and beat in the little cubes of butter, one at a time. Do not add the next piece of butter until the previous one has been fully absorbed. Season to taste with salt and pepper before serving.

You can keep the sauce warm for up to 1 hour by setting the bowl in a pan of water that is kept just above lukewarm – if it is allowed to become too hot, the sauce will curdle; if too cold, it will begin to harden.

There is a short-cut way of making this sauce which is almost as good: put the egg yolks, lemon juice and water into a blender until smooth. Heat the butter in a saucepan until it just begins to froth, then, keeping the blender at full speed, slowly drip in the butter until it has all been absorbed and the sauce has thickened. Season to taste with salt and pepper before serving.

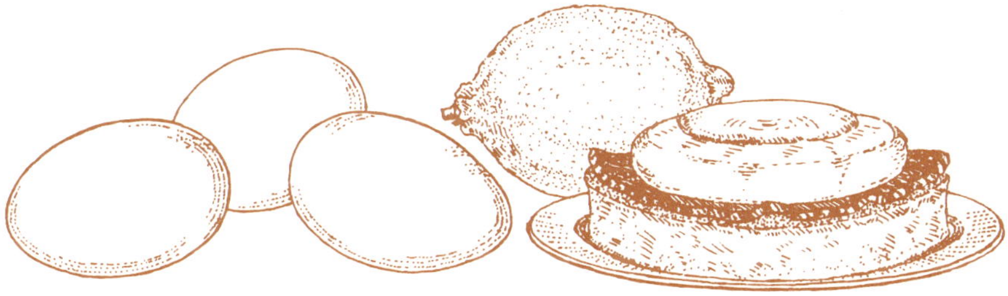

Sauce Béarnaise *Herbed Butter Sauce*

BEARN

This sauce is not really a native of Béarn, but it is said to have been invented for Henri IV and named after his native land. It is excellent with chicken, steak or fish.

Preparation time: 20 minutes
Cooking time: 15 to 20 minutes

To serve: 6

5 tablespoons wine vinegar
5 tablespoons water
2 fresh tarragon branches
2 shallots, finely chopped
1 strip of lemon rind
6 peppercorns, lightly crushed
3 egg yolks
175 g/6 oz unsalted butter, diced

Put the vinegar and water into a small saucepan, add the tarragon, shallots, lemon rind and peppercorns and boil fiercely until the liquid is reduced to about 2 tablespoons. Strain.

Put the egg yolks into a heatproof bowl and beat until thick and fluffy. Beat in the liquid. Place the bowl over a pan of simmering water and slowly add the butter, piece by piece, beating each one in until absorbed before adding the next. Season to taste with salt and pepper before serving.

You can also use a short-cut method of making this sauce, using the method given for sauce hollandaise on page 113.

Pâte Brisée *Shortcrust Pastry*

This is the standard French pastry for quiches and tarts. It is light and crisp, and should be handled as little and as lightly as possible. The proportion of fat to flour is very high, and the pastry is consequently rather fragile. You can, of course, vary this proportion a little, but the pastry will not be quite as delicate.

The following quantities make sufficient dough to line two 25 to 30 cm/10 to 12 inch flan tins. The dough keeps in the refrigerator for at least a week, or for about 3 months in the freezer.

Preparation time: 10 minutes (plus 1 hour resting)

150 g/5½ oz flour
pinch of salt
pinch of icing sugar
100 g/4 oz butter, preferably unsalted
a little iced water

Sift the flour onto a pastry board together with the salt and icing sugar. Cut the butter into small pieces and cut into the flour with a palette knife, then rub in with the fingertips until the mixture resembles fine breadcrumbs. Sprinkle with a little iced water, then gather together into a ball with one hand.

Sprinkle a little flour onto the board and, using the heel of your hand, quickly spread the dough away from you onto the floured board. This will ensure that the butter is evenly distributed. This whole operation should be done as quickly and lightly as possible. Gather up into a ball again and leave in the refrigerator to rest for at least 1 hour.

Leave the dough at room temperature for a little while before rolling out, so that it becomes malleable again. If it is very hard at first, hit it with a rolling pin, but do not knead again.

Pâte Brisée Sucrée

Sweetened Shortcrust Pastry

Make this in the same way as the pâte brisée, but instead of adding only a pinch of icing sugar, add 50 g/2 oz of icing or caster sugar.

Gougère

BURGUNDY

Served with a good bottle of red Burgundy, this simple dish makes an excellent first course, or a light lunch or supper dish. To make it more substantial, you can fill the centre with a delicate green vegetable, covered with a sauce hollandaise (see page *113*).

Preparation time: 20 minutes
Cooking time: 35 to 40 minutes
Oven temperature: 190°C, 375°F, Gas Mark 5
To serve: 4 to 6

300 ml/½ pint milk
100 g/4 oz butter
salt
white pepper
125 g/4½ oz plain flour, sifted
4 eggs
100 g/4 oz Gruyère or Comté cheese, diced

Gougère

Put the milk into a heavy saucepan together with the butter cut into small pieces and salt and pepper to taste. Heat slowly, stirring, until the butter has melted, then bring rapidly to the boil to combine. As soon as the milk is boiling, take the pan off the heat and tip in all the flour. Stir rapidly with a wooden spoon to form a smooth paste. Return to a moderate heat, stir until the mixture forms a ball and leaves the sides of the pan clean.

Take off the heat and beat in the eggs one by one. When the last egg has been absorbed and the mixture is smooth and glossy, stir in all but 1 tablespoon of the diced cheese.

Butter a ring mould or savarin pan and spoon in the mixture evenly. Scatter the remaining cheese over the top.

Bake in the oven until the top has risen, is golden brown and just firm to the touch. Turn out of the mould carefully and serve immediately, very hot.

Pâte Feuilletée *Puff Pastry*

Although ready-made bought puff pastry can be used for all the recipes requiring pâte feuilletée, it takes only a little while to learn to make this 'pastry of a thousand leaves' yourself, and the effort is very worthwhile, as the results are infinitely more melting on the tongue. If at first you don't achieve the desired standard of perfection, do try again – it is a knack you will learn.

The dough keeps in the refrigerator for at least a week, or 3–4 months in the freezer.

Preparation time: 30 minutes (plus 4 to 5 hours resting)
Makes: about 0.75 kg/1½ lb

0.5 kg/1 lb plain flour
½ teaspoon salt
2 tablespoons corn or nut oil
about 150 ml/¼ pint iced water
175 g/6 oz butter, preferably unsalted

Sift the flour and salt into a mixing bowl, sprinkle on the oil and most of the water, and begin to mix with a wooden spoon or spatula. Start to gather up the dough with one hand, sprinkling on a little more water as necessary to make a workable dough, but not one that is damp or sticky. When you have a ball of dough, sprinkle it with a little flour and leave to rest in the refrigerator for 30 minutes.

Remove from the refrigerator and roll or pat out into a rectangle three times as long as it is wide on a lightly floured surface.

Place the butter between two sheets of greaseproof or wax paper and beat it into a flat rectangle, using a rolling pin. Place the butter on a lightly floured surface, sprinkle with more flour and work it into smooth, pliable consistency, using the ball of the hand. Spread the butter onto the two thirds of the dough furthest away from you, leaving a narrow margin all round.

Fold the third that is nearest to you over towards the centre and then fold over again. Give the parcel a quarter turn. Sprinkle the working surface and the dough with a little flour and roll out firmly away from yourself to form another long rectangle. Fold both ends of the rectangle towards the centre, then fold over to make a neat parcel. Refrigerate the dough for about 1 hour.

Repeat the process of twice rolling and folding the dough once more.

Let the dough rest a few minutes at room temperature when you take it out of the refrigerator, and if it still seems too firm to roll out at first, beat it lightly with the rolling pin before rolling out. After the fourth turn refrigerate the dough again for at least 1 hour before using.

Fondue Aux Trois Fromages *Cheese Fondue*

FRANCHE-COMTE

You need a fondue set, or at least a spirit lamp with a trivet that will hold your casserole on the table, to serve this dish, which is not just a meal but also an entertainment. Cheese fondues are eaten in Switzerland, as well as in the Franche-Comté and in the Savoie – the only slight difference is in the local cheeses used. If the selection of cheeses given below is unobtainable, use whatever hard, melting cheeses are available. When the fondue is ready it is set in the centre of the table, over a spirit flame. Everyone has a long-handled fork on which to spear the cubes of bread and dip them into the fondue.

Preparation time: 15 minutes
Cooking time: 20 minutes
To serve: 6

1 garlic clove, halved
225 g/8 oz Comté cheese, thinly sliced
225 g/8 oz Gruyère cheese, thinly sliced
225 g/8 oz Beaufort cheese, thinly sliced
300 ml/½ pint white wine
freshly ground black pepper
1 teaspoon cornflour
3 tablespoons kirsch
8 to 12 slices of day old white bread, cubed, for serving

Rub the clove of garlic firmly around the inside of a flameproof casserole. Put the cheeses and the wine into the casserole and stir over a moderate heat until all the cheese has melted. Season liberally with pepper.

Stir the cornflour and kirsch together to make a smooth paste. Add to the casserole and stir until you have a smooth, well combined cream. Bring to the boil, then transfer, still gently bubbling, to the spirit lamp on the table.

The fondue will continue to cook gently as you eat, and the mixture will get thicker as you get lower in the dish. Add a little more kirsch at the end if you like.

The thin crust which will have formed on the bottom of the casserole is a special *bonne bouche* and should be shared equally between the participants.

Fondue De Fromage A Brillat-Savarin *Cheese and Egg Fondue*

SAVOIE

Brillat-Savarin is one of the most famous names in French gastronomy. He was a native of the Savoie, and his recipes and preferences often reflect the influence of that heritage. His classic work *The Psychology of Taste* (1826) was more a celebration of good living and good food than a conventional cook book. This recipe is an approximation of a dish he describes, and would serve for a late supper or snack.

Preparation time: 10 minutes
Cooking time: 15 minutes
To serve: 6

12 eggs
150 g/5 oz butter
275 g/10 oz Gruyère cheese, finely grated
salt
freshly ground black pepper
toast (optional)

Break the eggs into a heavy saucepan and beat thoroughly. Melt the butter, cool slightly and add to the eggs. Stir in the grated cheese. Place the saucepan over a high heat and begin stirring the fondue vigorously with a wooden spoon. After a few minutes, turn the heat down slightly, but continue stirring. When the mixture begins thickening, watch it carefully so that it does not stick. Add a pinch of salt and plenty of pepper just before the fondue reaches the desired consistency. It will appear like slightly more granular scrambled eggs. Serve on toast or – alternatively and more classically – by itself on heated plates. Accompany with French bread, pickled onions and a green salad.

Sorbets, Fruit Desserts and Sweets

Coeur A La Crème *Cream Cheese Dessert*

NORMANDY

Light, delicate and refreshing, this may be eaten with cream, or with soft summer fruit. This dessert takes its name from the small heart-shaped white porcelain colanders in which it was originally made.

Preparation time: 20 minutes (plus draining overnight)
To serve: 4 to 6

225 g/8 oz curd or cottage cheese
300 ml/½ pint crème fraîche (see page 118)
25 g/1 oz caster sugar
2 egg whites
300 ml/½ pint single cream for serving

Pass the cheese through a nylon sieve. Lightly whip the cream with the sugar and mix into the cheese. Beat the egg whites until stiff and fold into the cheese mixture. Turn into the muslin, cheesecloth or paper towel lined mould, colander or sieve. Leave to drain overnight in the refrigerator.

Turn out, pour over the cream and serve.

Crème Fraîche *Lightly Soured Cream*

NORMANDY

In France cream is generally left to mature so that the lactic acids remain active and give it a very slightly sour taste. It is known as crème fraiche and is particularly good for cooking, as it lends a slight tang to savoury dishes, and acts as a very good thickener. It keeps better than fresh cream – 10 to 14 days in the refrigerator – though it will become thicker as time goes on.

Preparation time: 5 to 10 minutes (plus thickening)
Makes: about 600 ml/1 pint

2 tablespoons soured cream or buttermilk
600 ml/1 pint double cream

Stir the soured cream or buttermilk into the cream and heat very gently until lukewarm. The cream should still feel slightly cool to the back of the finger – the correct maximum temperature is 29°C/85°F. Pour into an earthenware bowl, cover and leave in a warm place to thicken. This will take from 5 to 24 hours, depending on the temperature. Refrigerate.

Note: If crème fraîche is not available when called for in recipes, it can be replaced by double cream, lightly soured with a little lemon juice, or by a mixture of double cream and soured cream.

Sorbet De Champagne *Champagne Sorbet*

CHAMPAGNE

This is a light and refreshing way to end a very special meal on a festive occasion.

Preparation time: 10 minutes (plus 3 hours minimum freezing)
Cooking time: 5 minutes
To serve: 6

600 ml/1 pint water
225 g/8 oz sugar
1 vanilla pod
finely pared rind and juice of 1 lemon
600 ml/1 pint Champagne
12 langues de chats for serving

Put the water, sugar, vanilla pod and lemon rind in a saucepan and bring to the boil, stirring to dissolve the sugar. Boil for 5 minutes. Strain and leave to cool.

Add the lemon juice and turn into an ice-tray. Put into the freezing compartment of the refrigerator, set at its coldest, or into the freezer. Freeze until set but still soft and mushy.

Turn into a chilled bowl and mash lightly with a fork until smooth. Mix in the Champagne. Return quickly to the freezer or refrigerator and leave until frozen.

Serve straight from the freezer in chilled Champagne glasses, accompanied by langues de chats.

Coeur à la crème and crème fraîche

Mousse Au Chocolat *Chocolate Mousse*

ILE DE FRANCE

Chocolat Menier, one of the best of cooking chocolates, has been made in a factory at Noisiel on the Marne, not far from Paris, since the house was founded in 1825. Use Menier chocolate if you can for this extremely simple and unfailingly popular recipe, and make the mousse a day ahead to give it time to settle, and for the flavour to mature.

Preparation time: 30 minutes (plus chilling)
To serve: 6

200 g/7 oz plain or bitter chocolate, broken into pieces
6 eggs, separated
2 tablespoons brandy
150 ml/$\frac{1}{4}$ pint whipped cream to decorate (optional)

Put the chocolate into a large heatproof bowl, set this over a pan of simmering water and leave until the chocolate has melted. Remove the bowl from the heat and beat in the egg yolks one by one with a wooden spoon. The mixture will be very stiff at first, but it will become soft and smooth as you continue to add the yolks. Stir in the brandy.

Beat the egg whites until they are stiff but not dry. Stir one-third into the chocolate mixture until completely combined, then lightly fold the chocolate mixture into the remaining egg whites, using a spatula or metal spoon. Pour into a serving dish and refrigerate overnight.

You can decorate the mousse with swirls of whipped cream before serving if you wish.

Cotignac Orléannais *Quince Paste*

ORLEANNAIS

This beautiful, opaque, deep amber pink quince paste is a speciality of the town of Orléans. It may be kept in sterilized jars, like a preserve, or in the freezer. It can be eaten alone, or with a little crème chantilly (see page 121), and it is especially good served with cream cheese or coeur à la crème (see page 118).

Preparation time: about 1 hour
Cooking time: about $2\frac{1}{2}$ hours

3 kg/7 lb quinces
2 large oranges
about 1 kg/2 lb sugar

Quarter and core half the quinces and cut them into small chunks. Put them in a large saucepan. Add enough water to cover, bring to the boil and simmer for about 1 hour, or until soft. Strain through a jelly bag or muslin-lined sieve, squeezing out as much juice as possible.

Peel, core and slice the remaining quinces. Put them into a clean saucepan with the quince juice. Cut the oranges in half, scoop out the flesh and squeeze out any remaining juice. Add the flesh and juice to the quinces, with enough water to come just to the top of the fruit mixture. Bring to the boil and simmer until very soft and almost puréed.

Liquidize the quince purée in a blender and then pass through a nylon sieve, so that no gritty parts remain. Weigh the purée and return to the clean saucepan with an equal quantity of sugar. Cook over a moderate heat, stirring frequently to prevent it from catching on the bottom of the pan, until the purée is very thick and beginning to come away from the sides of the saucepan. Cool and store in sterilized jars or freezer containers.

Crème Chantilly Whipped Cream

ILE DE FRANCE

The little town of Chantilly, some few miles north of Paris, famous for its rich pastures, has become associated forever with the lightly whipped, slightly soured cream that tops the best pâtisseries and desserts throughout France. Made with crème fraiche it has a pleasing slight acidity. Because crème fraiche can become very stiff, iced water needs to be added before it can be whipped, and it becomes therefore very light and airy, and much more delicate than our whipped cream.

Preparation time: 10 to 15 minutes

300 ml/$\frac{1}{2}$ pint crème fraiche (see page 118)
2 to 4 tablespoons iced water
about 2 teaspoons vanilla sugar or icing sugar
1 egg white, stiffly beaten (optional)

Whip the crème fraiche with a balloon whisk, adding the water gradually according to how stiff the cream is. Whip in sugar to taste towards the end, but remember that the cream should not be really sweet. If you want to use the cream in large quantities, you can fold in the stiffly beaten egg white at the end.

Crème chantilly may be put on the table in bowls so that everyone can serve themselves, or piped onto desserts in decorative patterns.

Petits Pots Au Chocolat Chocolate Creams

ILE DE FRANCE

These individual creams take their name from the little pot-bellied, two-handled pots, brown on the outside and white inside, in which they are traditionally served. The cream is very quick and simple to make, and is a perfect ending for a special meal. Although light, it is quite rich, and this quantity serves 4 generously.

Preparation time: 10 minutes (plus setting)
Cooking time: 3 minutes
To serve: 4

300 ml/$\frac{1}{2}$ pint single cream
200 g/7 oz plain or bitter chocolate, broken into pieces
pinch of salt
1 teaspoon vanilla essence
1 egg, beaten

Heat the cream to almost boiling point. Remove from the heat and add the chocolate. Stir until the chocolate has completely melted and the mixture is quite smooth. Add the salt and vanilla and stir in the egg.

Alternatively, if you have a blender, pour the cream, just off the boil, onto the chocolate in the blender goblet and blend until smooth. Blend in the remaining ingredients.

Pour into the individual pots and leave to set for at least 4 hours in the refrigerator.

Poires Au Cassis *Pears in Cassis*

BURGUNDY

An unusual and refreshing way of preparing pears, this uses the local blackcurrant liqueur.

Preparation time: 15 minutes (plus chilling)
Cooking time: 15 to 30 minutes
To serve: 6

6 large pears
225 g/8 oz sugar
450 ml/$\frac{3}{4}$ pint water
1 vanilla pod
150 ml/$\frac{1}{4}$ pint crème de cassis
juice of $\frac{1}{2}$ to 1 lemon

Peel the pears, leaving them whole and as far as possible with the stalks on.

Bring the sugar and water to the boil in a wide saucepan, stirring until the sugar has dissolved. Add the vanilla pod. Lower the pears gently into the syrup. They should all be covered by the liquid, so add a little more water if necessary. Simmer gently until the pears are tender, but take care not to overcook, as they must not be allowed to disintegrate.

When done, lift the pears out gently with a slotted spoon and place in a serving dish. Pour over the cassis.

Bring the syrup left in the pan to the boil and boil fiercely to reduce to about half the original quantity. Add lemon juice to taste and pour over the pears. Chill before serving.

Oeufs A La Neige

Poached Meringues with Custard

BURGUNDY

This delicate dessert is much loved by children. To make it more sophisticated you can sprinkle it with finely crushed praline.

Preparation time: 40 minutes (plus chilling)
Cooking time: 30 minutes
To serve: 4 to 6

4 eggs, separated
150 g/5 oz caster sugar
600 ml/1 pint milk
2 tablespoons water
1 vanilla pod

Beat the egg whites until they stand in peaks. Slowly beat in 75 g/3 oz of the sugar and continue to beat until very stiff.

Put the milk, water and vanilla pod in a wide saucepan and heat to just below boiling point. Using a large tablespoon, shape the mixture into large egg shapes. Float these on top of the milk, a few at a time. After 2 minutes, turn them over and poach on the other side. Lift out with a slotted spoon and leave to drain in a wide dish.

When all the meringue mixture has been used, remove the vanilla pod from the milk. Beat the egg yolks with the remaining sugar, then slowly beat in a little of the milk. Stir this mixture into the milk in the saucepan and stir over a very low heat until the custard thickens. Pour the custard into a shallow serving dish, and top with the meringue 'snowballs'. Chill before serving.

Sorbet De Raisins *Grape Sorbet*

BURGUNDY

Made with ripe, sweet table grapes, this is the perfect dessert to end a rich meal. It is light, refreshing, but by no means innocent!

Preparation time: 10 minutes (plus freezing)
Cooking time: 5 minutes
To serve: 4 to 6

0.75 kg/$1\frac{1}{2}$ lb black grapes
100 g/4 oz sugar (or a little more if the grapes are not very sweet)
300 ml/$\frac{1}{2}$ pint water
squeeze of lemon juice
2 tablespoons eau-de-vie de marc

Pluck the grapes off the stalks but do not bother to peel or seed. Put them into a blender and blend very briefly, then press through a nylon sieve to obtain all the juice and a little of the bitter flavour of the skins.

Put the sugar and water in a saucepan and bring to the boil, stirring to dissolve the sugar. Boil for 5 minutes. Cool, then stir into the grape juice. Add a little lemon juice and taste for sweetness – the mixture should taste a little over-sweet at this point. Pour into freezing trays and freeze.

When the mixture begins to set, mash it lightly with a fork or in a blender and blend in the marc. Return to the freezer and freeze until hard, a minimum of 2 hours.

Serve in chilled wine glasses, straight from the freezer.

Poires au cassis, poirat de Berry (page 141), souffle glace au kirsch (page 125) and ouefs à la neige

Gelée De Groseilles *Redcurrant Jelly*

LORRAINE

The sunripened redcurrants of Lorraine make wonderful jams and jellies, and these are used as much for cooking as to spread on 'tartines'. Fruit tarts, in particular, are often glazed with a jelly made of the same fruit, or of one with contrasting flavour or colour.

Preparation time: 30 minutes (plus straining overnight)
Cooking time: 5 to 10 minutes

redcurrants
sugar

Wash the redcurrants. Put into a preserving pan with just enough water to stop them catching. Bring slowly to the boil. Stir and lightly mash the fruit as it heats.

Remove the fruit from the heat and pour into a scalded jelly bag. Allow to drip through overnight. Measure the juice and allow 1 kg, just over 2 lb sugar, to each 1 litre/$1\frac{3}{4}$ pints of juice. Put into the preserving pan and bring very slowly to the boil, stirring all the time so that the sugar dissolves evenly. Do not let it boil until the sugar has dissolved.

Boil for 5 minutes without stirring, then test by dropping a little of the jelly onto a cold saucer. When a skin forms as it cools, the jelly is ready.

Leave to cool a little in the pan, then remove any scum and pour into sterilized small jars. Seal and keep in a cool place.

Gelée De Groseilles A Froid *Uncooked Redcurrant Jelly*

LORRAINE

These translucent jellies are potted in very small quantities in miniature glass jars, and kept as a great delicacy. They do not keep as well as the cooked jelly, but their flavour is quite miraculous, and small quantities, melted down to make a glaze or used in small blobs as decoration, transform a dessert. This recipe is only suitable for use when redcurrants are very plentiful and ripe.

Preparation time: 1 hour (plus straining overnight)

redcurrants, washed and stripped off the stalks
caster sugar

Put the redcurrants into a large bowl and crush them very gently with a wooden mallet or spoon. Put the contents of the bowl into a scalded jelly bag and allow to drip through overnight. Weigh the juice and weigh out an equal quantity of sugar. Add the sugar little by little to the currant juice, stirring all the time so that the sugar dissolves. When all the sugar has dissolved, pour into small sterilized jars, cover and keep in a light, dry place.

Les Groseilles Au Jus De Framboise *Redcurrants in Raspberry Juice*

ALSACE

This is a lovely tart, refreshing dessert. Its jewel colours look wonderful served in sparkling glasses on a sunny day.

Preparation time: 15 minutes (plus chilling)
Cooking time: 5 minutes
To serve: 4 to 6

0.5 kg/1 lb redcurrants (or red and white currants mixed), stripped off the stalks
225 g/8 oz raspberries
150 g/5 oz sugar
squeeze of lemon juice

Pile the currants into individual long-stemmed wine glasses.

Put the raspberries and sugar into a heavy saucepan, crush them lightly and heat gently, so that the juice begins to run. Do not boil, as this alters the flavour of the fruit.

Pass the raspberry juice through a nylon sieve. Add the lemon juice and a little more sugar if necessary, depending on how tart the currants are. Pour the raspberry sauce over the currants in the glasses, chill and serve.

Sorbet De Framboises Et De Groseilles *Raspberry and Redcurrant Ice*

ALSACE

French sorbets tend to be very light but slightly creamy – somewhere halfway between the Italian water ices and the English ice creams. This is a particularly delicate and refreshing combination of fruit flavours.

Preparation time: 20 minutes (plus 2 hours minimum freezing)
Cooking time: 5 minutes
To serve: 6

about 350 g/12 oz raspberries
about 150 g/5 oz redcurrants
150 g/5 oz sugar
150 ml/$\frac{1}{4}$ pint water
150 ml/$\frac{1}{4}$ pint crème fraîche (see page 118) or single cream

Purée the raspberries and redcurrants together in a blender, then pass through a nylon sieve.

Dissolve the sugar in the water in a saucepan, then bring to the boil. Boil vigorously for 5 minutes, to make a syrup. Cool.

Stir the cooled syrup into the fruit purée followed by the cream and pour into a freezing tray. Put into the freezing compartment of the refrigerator, set at its coldest, or into the freezer.

When the mixture begins to set, remove it from the freezer and beat well, preferably with an electric beater or in a blender. Return to the freezer and leave to set.

Remove from the freezer and keep in the refrigerator for 1 hour before serving.

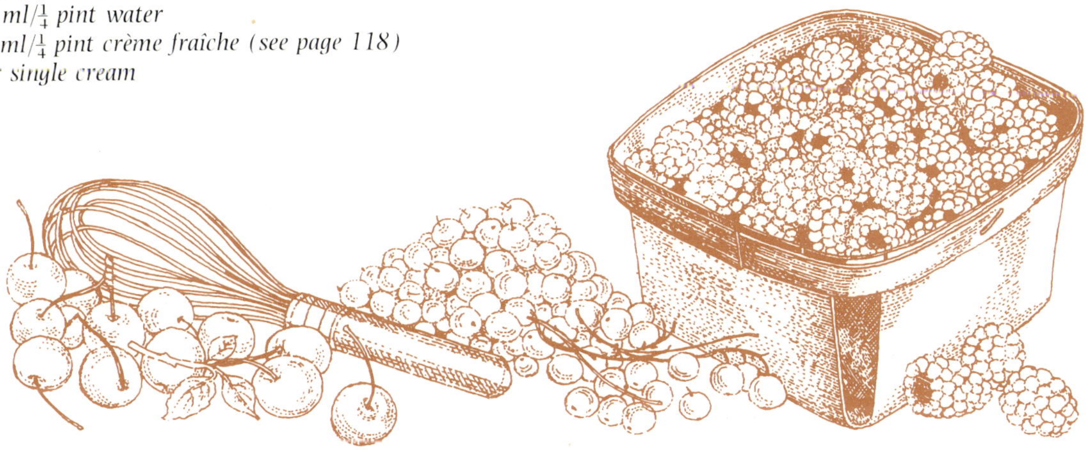

Soufflé Glacé Au Kirsch *Iced Kirsch Soufflé*

FRANCHE-COMTE

Kirschwasser, the eau-de-vie made from cherries, is the product of the Black Forest and the Vosges, the forested mountain regions that border France, and is used quite extensively in cooking in this part of France also. The following is a wonderfully rich but light dessert.

Preparation time: 20 minutes (plus freezing)
Cooking time: 3 to 5 minutes
To serve: 6

225 g/8 oz sugar
150 ml/$\frac{1}{4}$ pint water
4 egg whites
2 tablespoons Kirschwasser
300 ml/$\frac{1}{2}$ pint crème fraîche (see page 118) or double cream

Dissolve the sugar in the water in a saucepan, then bring to the boil. Boil for 3 to 5 minutes or until a thick syrup is formed. Beat the egg whites until they stand in peaks, and, continuing to beat, pour in the syrup in a thin stream. Dribble in the Kirschwasser.

Whip the cream lightly until it is thick and bulky but not stiff. Fold into the soufflé mixture. Pour into a freezerproof glass serving dish and freeze until set.

Serve frozen.

Glace Au Miel *Honey Ice-Cream*

PROVENCE

The herb-scented honeys of Provence give this ice-cream a marvellous flavour. Unless you have one of these special honeys, it is worth using some fresh herbs to achieve the same tangy sweetness.

Preparation time: 20 minutes (plus 4 hours minimum freezing)
Cooking time: 10 minutes
To serve: 6

6 egg yolks
150 ml/¼ pint honey
1 fresh rosemary or thyme branch
300 ml/½ pint milk or single cream
150 ml/¼ pint crème fraîche (see page 118), double or whipping cream

Beat the egg yolks until they are light and fluffy.

Heat the honey together with the rosemary or thyme until it just reaches boiling point. Remove the herb and pour the honey onto the yolks, beating well.

Bring the milk or cream to just below boiling point and beat this into the honey mixture. Pour into a heavy saucepan and stir over a very gentle heat until the mixture begins to thicken. On no account allow it to boil. Remove from the heat and leave to cool.

Whip the cream until thick and bulky and fold into the cooled honey custard. Turn into a freezing tray or serving dish and freeze.

Remove from the freezer 15 minutes before serving.

Compôte De Fruits D'Hiver *Winter Fruit Salad*

PROVENCE

While Provence is a summer paradise, the winters can be cold and biting. A salad like this one, with its memory of the fruits of summer, can be very cheering.

Preparation time: 20 minutes (plus soaking)
Cooking time: 30 to 40 minutes
To serve: 6

100 g/4 oz prunes, soaked overnight, drained and stoned
100 g/4 oz dried apricots, soaked overnight and drained
100 g/4 oz dried peaches, soaked overnight and drained
4 small cooking pears, peeled
300 ml/½ pint red wine
1 cinnamon stick
2 cloves
1 vanilla pod
about 50 g/2 oz sugar
1 orange, peeled and sliced
6 walnuts, shelled and halved

Put all the prepared fruits except the orange into a heavy wide-bottomed saucepan and add the wine, spices, sugar and enough water just to cover the fruit. Poach until the fruit is tender.

Lift the fruit out with a slotted spoon and place in a serving dish. Add the orange slices and the walnut halves.

Bring the poaching liquid to the boil and boil rapidly until reduced by about half. Add more sugar to taste, strain over the fruit and leave to cool before serving.

Glace au miel, croquante and compote de fruits d'hiver

Croquante Almond Brittle

PROVENCE

One of the traditional Christmas desserts of Provence, this is made in large sheets and sometimes shaped over a bowl to make a *cloche* or bell shape. This is then placed on the table and everyone can break off a piece as they wish.

If the mixture is simply left to cool and harden, it can be crushed to form a praline powder, to be used to flavour desserts and ices, or to decorate cakes.

Preparation time: 20 minutes
Cooking time: 10 minutes
Oven temperature: 180°C, 350°F, Gas Mark 4
To serve: 6

0.5 kg/1 lb almonds, blanched and roughly chopped
225 g/8 oz sugar, brown or white, or a mixture of the two
6 tablespoons water

Toast the almonds gently in the oven or brown lightly under the grill, until just pale golden brown.

Put the sugar into a heavy saucepan with the water and bring very gently to the boil, stirring until all the sugar has dissolved. Boil until the syrup reaches a temperature of 150°C/300°F or until it turns golden brown. If you are using brown sugar, it is best to use a sweet thermometer, as the colour is deceptive.

Remove from the heat and add the almonds. Stir well so that they become evenly coated with the caramel. Pour quickly onto an oiled wooden board, and use the back of a wooden spoon to spread out as thinly as possible. You need to work fast as the mixture hardens quickly.

To make a bell shape, lift the sheet of brittle off as soon as it has set and mould over the back of a bowl. Remove the bowl and leave to cool.

If praline is needed, crush into a powder when the mixture is quite cold and hard.

Nougat *Honey and Almond Candy*

DAUPHINE

This is a speciality of the town of Montélimar, which borders on Provence, and indeed this confection relies on some of the products of Provence, with its herb and flower-scented honeys and pink-blossomed almond trees. In Montélimar you will see boxes of nougat in the confectioners' windows all the year through, but further south, in Nice, where they have their own version of nougat, it is a traditional part of the Christmas celebrations.

It is not difficult to master the art of making nougat, although a sweet thermometer is probably essential. Once mastered, it is a most enjoyable pre-Christmas occupation.

Preparation time: 15 minutes (plus setting)
Cooking time: about 40 minutes
Oven temperature: 190°C, 375°F, Gas Mark 5 (optional)

175 g/6 oz blanched almonds, roughly chopped
2 egg whites
100 g/4 oz honey
100 g/4 oz sugar
2 tablespoons water
rice paper

Toast the almonds lightly under a grill or in the oven.

Whisk the egg whites until they form soft peaks.

Heat the honey in a small heavy saucepan to 150°C/300°F. In another saucepan, heat the sugar and water, stirring until the sugar has dissolved, then bring to the boil and boil until the syrup also reaches 150°C/300°F. Mix the honey and syrup together. Carefully stir in the egg whites. Add the nuts, then slowly bring to the boil. Boil for 1 minute.

Line a loaf pan with foil and then with a sheet of rice paper. Pour in the nougat mixture, cover with another sheet of rice paper and weigh down. Leave at room temperature to cool and set for at least 12 hours before cutting into small squares or bars. Eat while fresh.

Parfait Marie Brizard *Iced Anisette Mousse*

GUYENNE

Marie Brizard is the local liqueur made from aniseed, and it has a highly sophisticated flavour.

Preparation time: 20 minutes (plus freezing)
Cooking time: 5 minutes
To serve: 6

100 g/4 oz sugar
300 ml/$\frac{1}{2}$ pint water
4 large egg yolks
4 tablespoons Marie Brizard
450 ml/$\frac{3}{4}$ pint whipping cream

Dissolve the sugar in the water in a saucepan and bring to the boil. Boil briskly for 5 minutes.

Meanwhile beat the egg yolks with an electric beater until they are fluffy. Pour in the very hot sugar syrup in a thin stream and continue to beat at full speed until the mixture is cool. Beat in the Marie Brizard.

Whip the cream lightly, then fold into the egg mixture. Pour into a freezerproof serving dish or individual ramekin dishes and freeze for at least 4 hours.

Serve straight from the freezer.

Cakes, Crêpes and Patisseries

Les Crêpes Dentellées *Lacy Pancakes*

BRITTANY

If Brittany has a national dish, it must be crêpes, the huge buckwheat pancakes which can be bought at every street corner, to be eaten wrapped around a piece of local sausage, a lump of cheese, or with butter and sugar or jam. Crêperies are to be found in every little Breton town, and in these small restaurants you can make a whole meal of crêpes, washed down with the local cider, starting with savoury fillings, such as seafood, ham or chicken, and working your way through cheese and fruit to a final crêpe au chocolat.

These buckwheat pancakes, though good if you are very hungry, can be rather heavy, and more attractive are the lacy little crêpes dentellées, the speciality of the town of Quimper.

Preparation time: 10 minutes
Cooking time: 20 minutes
To serve: 4 to 6

100 g/4 oz flour
50 g/2 oz icing sugar
pinch of salt
1 large egg, lightly beaten
25 g/1 oz butter, melted and cooled
1 tablespoon vegetable oil
1 tablespoon brandy
about 150 ml/$\frac{1}{4}$ pint warm water
oil for frying
sugar and orange or lemon juice for serving

Sift the flour, sugar and salt into a bowl, make a well in the centre and add the egg, butter, oil and brandy. Gradually work the flour into the liquids, adding enough of the water to make a smooth, fairly thin batter.

Cook in a lightly oiled hot pan, to make small and very thin crêpes. As soon as the batter touches the frying pan, it will begin to form bubbles, which then become holes, making the crêpes look like lacy doilies.

Sprinkle with sugar and a little orange or lemon juice to serve.

Tarte Normande, pain perdu Normand and bourdelats Normands (page 132)

Gâteau Breton *Breton Cake*

BRITTANY

This lovely plain but buttery cake is sold at street corners and in markets all over Brittany, and you can buy a slice to eat at any time of day. Have it with a cup of tea or coffee – or do as the Bretons do, and drink a glass of dry country cider with it.

Preparation time: 20 minutes
Cooking time: 1 hour 20 minutes
Oven temperature: 190°C, 375°F, Gas Mark 5
To serve: 6 to 8

350 g/12 oz flour
175 g/6 oz caster sugar
6 egg yolks
200 g/7 oz butter, at room temperature

Sift the flour and sugar into a bowl and make a well in the centre. Beat 5 of the egg yolks together lightly with a fork. Pour into the well and slowly work in the flour, using a wooden spoon at first, and then your fingertips to crumble together finely.

Cut the butter into small pieces and, using a palette knife at first and then your fingertips, work them into the mixture until you have a fine, crumbly pastry. Press into a well-buttered 22 cm/9 inch flan tin. Brush over the top with the remaining egg yolk and trace a pattern with a fork.

Bake in the oven until the top is golden brown. Turn out and allow to cool before serving.

Pain Perdu Normand

Normandy Bread and Apple Dessert
NORMANDY

This delicious dessert is made very quickly with simple ingredients.

Preparation time: 10 minutes
Cooking time: 8 minutes
To serve: 4

6 to 8 slices of stale white bread or brioche
3 tablespoons cider
1 egg, beaten
50 g/2 oz butter
2 eating apples, peeled, cored and thinly sliced
2 tablespoons sugar
2 tablespoons Calvados

Spread out the slices of bread or brioche and sprinkle the cider over them. Leave to soak for a few minutes, then dip quickly into the egg so that both sides are lightly coated.

Melt the butter in a frying pan. When foaming, add the slices of bread and fry quickly on one side. Turn over and add the apples. When the bread is golden brown on both sides, sprinkle with the sugar, pour on the warmed Calvados and set alight. Bring flaming to the table.

Les crêpes dentilles and gateau Breton

Tarte Normande *Normandy Apple Tart*

NORMANDY

Of the dozens of ways of making apple tart known to the French housewife, this one uses the most apples – appropriately from a region famous for its apple orchards.

Preparation time: 30 minutes (plus pastry)
Cooking time: 35 minutes
Oven temperature: 220°C, 425°F, Gas Mark 7
To serve: 6

225 g/8 oz quantity pâte brisée sucrée (see page 114)
1 kg/2 lb cooking apples
about 150 ml/$\frac{1}{4}$ pint water
25 g/1 oz butter
50 g/2 oz sugar (or a little more)
2 tablespoons apricot jam, apple jelly or marmalade

Roll out the pâte brisée dough thinly and use to line a 30 cm/12 inch loose-bottomed, fluted flan tin. Prick all over and bake blind for 10 minutes.

Meanwhile, set aside 2 or 3 large apples; peel, core and chop the remainder. Cook the chopped apples with just enough water to stop them catching, until quite soft. Add the butter and sugar to taste (the mixture should still be quite tart) and beat to a smooth purée.

Peel, quarter and core the remaining apples and slice into transparently thin half moons.

Spread the apple purée in the pastry case and cover with the apple slices arranged in circles and tightly overlapping. Sprinkle with a little more sugar and bake in the top of the oven until the edges of the apple slices are just darkened.

When the tart has cooled, melt the jam, jelly or marmalade, strain it and brush over the apple slices to glaze the tart.

Bourdelots Normands *Baked Apples in Pastry Cases*

NORMANDY

A simple dessert, this is always popular with adults and children alike, and is sometimes known as 'apples in their dressing gowns'.

Preparation time: 15 minutes (plus pastry)
Cooking time: 40 to 45 minutes
Oven temperature: 220°C, 425°F, Gas Mark 7; reduced to 190°C, 375°F, Gas Mark 5
To serve: 4

100 g/4 oz icing sugar
50 g/2 oz butter
4 large eating apples, peeled and cored
225 g/8 oz quantity pâte feuilletée (see page 115) or puff pastry
1 egg yolk
1 tablespoon water
single cream for serving

Work all but 1 tablespoon of the sugar into the butter. Stuff the centre of each apple with this mixture.

Roll out the pâte feuilletée dough and cut into four large squares. Place an apple in the centre of each square, bring up the corners to make a neat parcel and seal the edges. Decorate with any scraps of leftover dough. Place on a buttered baking sheet.

Mix the egg yolk with the water and brush the outside of each parcel. Bake in the hot oven for 15 minutes, then reduce the temperature and bake for a further 25 to 30 minutes.

Sprinkle with the remaining sugar and serve warm, with cream.

Beignets De Fruits A La Lilloise *Fruit Fritters*

FLANDERS

Like most of the dishes of this region, this is a warming and sustaining dessert, but the batter is exceptionally light and delicious. You can use any number of differing fruits to add variety. Take care not to eat the fritters too quickly, as the fruits retain heat longer than the batter and it is easy to burn your tongue!

Preparation time: 30 minutes (plus 1 hour resting)
Cooking time: 20 to 30 minutes
To serve: 6 to 8

225 g/8 oz plain flour
pinch of salt
2 eggs
300 ml/½ pint beer
1 tablespoon vegetable oil
2 large eating apples, peeled, cored and sliced or cut into rings
2 bananas, cut into chunks
2 oranges, peeled and segmented
75 g/3 oz caster sugar
1 tablespoon brandy
2 egg whites
oil for deep frying

Sift the flour and salt into a bowl and make a well in the centre. Beat the 2 eggs with all but 2 tablespoons of the beer, pour into the centre of the bowl and work into a smooth batter. Add the oil and leave to rest for 1 hour.

Arrange the fruit on separate plates, sprinkle with 50 g/2 oz of the sugar and dribble on the remaining beer and the brandy. Leave to macerate while the batter is resting.

Beat the egg whites until stiff and fold into the batter.

Heat the frying oil to 150°C/300°F.

Drain the fruit. Dip first the banana chunks into the batter, drop into the hot oil and fry for 4 minutes, turning them over halfway through. Do the same with the apples and oranges, but give the apple fritters 6 minutes cooking time. Drain on paper towels and keep hot.

Sprinkle with the remaining sugar before serving.

Profiteroles Au Chocolat *Chocolate Profiteroles*

ILE DE FRANCE

Choux pastry is a product of the sheer genius of French cooking, and these airy puffs, filled with a delicate crème chantilly and lightly enrobed with bitter chocolate sauce, must be about the most perfect dessert – light but rich, sweet without being cloying.

Preparation time: 30 minutes
Cooking time: 25 minutes for the puffs, 5 minutes for the sauce
Oven temperature: 220°C, 425°F, Gas Mark 7
To serve: 6

Choux paste
300 ml/½ pint water
100 g/4 oz butter, preferably unsalted
pinch of salt
1 teaspoon sugar
125 g/4½ oz sifted flour
4 eggs
300 ml/½ pint crème chantilly (see page 121)

Sauce
150 ml/¼ pint water
1 tablespoon cocoa powder
200 g/7 oz plain or bitter chocolate, broken into pieces
15 g/½ oz butter

To make the choux paste put the water into a large saucepan, add the butter roughly cut into pieces, the salt and the sugar and bring slowly to the boil, stirring until the butter has melted. As soon as the water has come to the boil, take the saucepan off the heat and tip in all the flour. Beat with a wooden spoon until smooth, then return to a moderate heat and continue to beat until the mixture forms a ball and leaves the sides of the pan clean. Remove the pan from the heat again and beat in the eggs one by one, adding each only when the previous one has been completely absorbed.

Fill a piping bag fitted with a plain nozzle with the choux paste and pipe small mounds onto a greased baking sheet, or drop small mounds onto the baking sheet with a teaspoon, making them as smooth as possible.

Bake in the top of the hot oven until the puffs are well risen and pale brown. Remove the puffs from the oven and turn it off. Make an incision with the tip of a sharp knife in the side of each puff to let out the damp air. Lay each puff on its side on the baking sheet and return to the oven, leaving the oven door open. Dry for about 10 minutes, then cool on a wire rack.

When the puffs are quite cold and not too long before you are ready to serve them, fill each one with crème chantilly, and pile them in a serving dish.

Make the sauce by bringing the water and cocoa to the boil in a saucepan, stirring until smooth. Boil for 1 minute. Remove from the heat, add the chocolate and stir until the chocolate has melted. Add the butter cut into small pieces to give the sauce a glaze, and stir until smooth.

Pour the hot sauce over the profiteroles and serve.

Note: The profiteroles can also be filled with vanilla ice-cream, giving the added pleasure of the contrast of temperatures.

Tarte Tatin *Caramelized Apple Tart*

ORLEANNAIS

The Demoiselles Tatin who lived in the Sologne area are credited with this famous upside-down apple tart, which is delicious and really not difficult to make. Use tart eating apples, such as the French Reinettes, English Coxes, or American Mcintosh.

Preparation time: 20 minutes (plus pastry)
Cooking time: 35 to 40 minutes
Oven temperature: 200°C, 400°F, Gas Mark 6
To serve: 4

50 g/2 oz butter
100 g/4 oz sugar
500 g/1 lb apples, peeled, cored and thickly sliced
150 g/5 oz pâte brisée sucrée (see page 114)

Butter a 20 cm/8 inch flan tin thickly, using half the butter. Sprinkle with half the sugar. Arrange the apple slices closely in circles in the tin.

Place the tin over a fairly high, even heat (electricity or solid fuel are more suitable than gas for this operation) and heat for 5 minutes to allow the butter and sugar to melt and lightly caramelize. Remove from the heat, dot the apples with the remaining butter and sprinkle with the remaining sugar.

Roll out the dough to the size of the tin. Cover the apples with the dough, allowing the edges to fall just inside the tin. Make several incisions in the dough lid with the point of a sharp knife to allow steam to escape.

Bake in the moderately hot oven until the pastry is golden brown. Allow to cool a little before carefully turning out the tart by inverting it onto a large dish. Serve warm or cold.

Savarin Montmorency

Savarin with Cherries
ILE DE FRANCE

A savarin is one of the classics of French pâtisserie, a light yeast dough baked in a ring mould and impregnated to saturation point with an alcoholic syrup. It is not difficult to make, provided you give yourself the time to go through all the processes in an unhurried way. It can also be made well ahead, kept frozen, and warmed through in a gentle oven. The classic savarin is made with a rum- or kirsch-flavoured syrup and then decorated with blanched almonds and glacé cherries, and served with crème chantilly.

This particular version takes its name from the slightest tart cherries of Montmorency, a richly fertile orchard area outside Paris.

Preparation time: 2 hours minimum
Cooking time: 40 minutes
Oven temperature: 190°C, 375°F, Gas Mark 5
To serve: 6 to 8

Savarin
15 g/$\frac{1}{2}$ oz fresh yeast
25 g/1 oz sugar
225 g/8 oz plain flour
150 ml/$\frac{1}{4}$ pint lukewarm milk
pinch of salt
4 eggs
100 g/4 oz butter, melted

Filling
0.5 kg/1 lb tart cherries, stoned (or use canned Morello cherries)
sugar to taste
good squeeze of lemon juice
4 tablespoons kirsch
300 ml/$\frac{1}{2}$ pint crème chantilly (see page 121)

Savarin Montmorency

Cream the yeast with 1 teaspoon of the sugar and 1 teaspoon of the flour and stir in the milk. Leave in a warm place until frothy.

Sift the remaining flour and the salt into a large warmed bowl and make a well in the centre. Pour in the yeast mixture and gradually work in the flour. Beat with a wooden spoon or knead with a lightly floured hand until the dough becomes elastic and leaves the side of the bowl clean. Cover with a clean cloth and leave in a warm place to rise to twice its original volume.

Beat the eggs lightly together with the remaining sugar and add the melted butter. Slowly beat this mixture into the dough and continue to beat with a wooden spoon until the dough becomes smooth and glossy. Turn into a buttered 25 cm/10 inch savarin or ring mould and cover once more with a clean cloth. Leave to rise again in a warm place until the mixture comes to the top of the mould.

Bake in the moderately hot oven until the top of the savarin is lightly browned and firm to the touch, and it has shrunk away a little from the sides of the mould. Turn out onto a wire cake rack and leave to cool.

Meanwhile, put the cherries in a saucepan and add enough water to come halfway up the cherries. Simmer until soft. Add sugar to taste and a squeeze of lemon juice. Drain the cherries, reserving the syrup. Add 3 tablespoons of the kirsch to the syrup.

If you are using canned cherries, drain them and add the lemon juice and kirsch to the syrup.

While the savarin is still slightly warm, place the cake rack over a dish and gently spoon over the lightly warmed cherry syrup until the savarin is completely impregnated, soft and spongy; it must not lose its shape.

Transfer carefully to a serving dish and pour over any syrup that has been caught in the dish under the rack. Sprinkle with the remaining kirsch. Pile the cherries into the centre and top with a little of the crème chantilly. Serve the remaining crème chantilly separately.

Croissants

Sweet Crescents
ILE DE FRANCE

It is improbable that any French housewife would dream of baking her own croissants – after all, that is what the *boulanger* is there for. But for those with fond memories of breakfast and croissants in a Paris café, and no nearby source for croissants, they are well worth making at home. They are not difficult to make, but unless you want to stay up all night, they must be made at least a day ahead and either briefly reheated before serving or kept in the refrigerator overnight, and baked before breakfast in the morning. They also freeze well.

Preparation time: 1 day
Cooking time: 15 to 20 minutes
Oven temperature: 230°C, 450°F, Gas Mark 8
Makes: 10 to 12 large croissants

15 g/½ oz fresh yeast
2 tablespoons lukewarm water
25 g/1 oz sugar
250 g/9 oz strong plain flour
1 teaspoon salt
150 ml/¼ pint lukewarm milk
1 tablespoon corn oil
100 g/4 oz butter
1 egg yolk
2 tablespoons cold milk

Dissolve the yeast in the warm water with 1 teaspoon of the sugar. Leave in a warm place until frothy.

Sift 225 g/8 oz of the flour into a large warm bowl with the salt, make a well in the centre and pour in the yeast mixture. Add the warm milk with the remaining sugar dissolved in it, and the oil. Gently mix the flour into the liquid, then turn out onto a board lightly sprinkled with some of the remaining flour and knead very lightly, just until the dough begins to keep its shape. Use a plastic spatula if the dough is too soft to knead by hand and use as much of the rest of the flour on the board as necessary. Return the dough to the clean mixing bowl, cover with a clean cloth and leave in a fairly warm place for 3 to 4 hours or until it has risen to about three times its original volume.

Knock back the dough and leave to rise again for 1 to 2 hours, or until it has doubled in bulk.

When the dough is ready, flatten the butter between sheets of greaseproof or wax paper by beating it gently with a rolling pin.

Knock back the dough in the bowl, then place it on a lightly floured board and gently roll it into a rectangle three times as long as it is wide. Spread the butter over the two-thirds of the rectangle furthest away from you, leaving a 1 cm/½ inch margin. Fold the unbuttered third towards the centre, and then fold over again. Seal the edges.

Give the dough a half turn and roll out again into a rectangle. Fold into three once more, wrap loosely in a lightly floured plastic bag and leave in the refrigerator for 1 hour.

Take out of the refrigerator, deflate and leave for a few minutes at room temperature, then roll out into a rectangle and fold into three again. Replace in the refrigerator for at least another hour.

When the dough is ready, divide it in half and roll out the first half on a lightly floured board into a rectangle just under 5 mm/¼ inch thick and about 15 cm/6 inches wide. Cut the dough into squares, and each square into a triangle. Take the wide edge of one triangle and roll it over towards the point. Stretch the point a little to lengthen it, so that it can wrap right around the roll. Place on a lightly greased baking sheet with the point tucked underneath and bring the two ends slightly around towards each other to form a crescent shape. Repeat with the remaining dough.

Leave the prepared croissants in a warm place until they have risen to twice their size and feel springy to the touch. Mix the egg yolk with the milk and brush this glaze over the croissants. Bake in the oven for 15 to 20 minutes.

The prepared uncooked croissants may also be left in the refrigerator overnight. Leave at room temperature for 30 minutes before baking.

Croissants

Linzertorte *Spiced Raspberry Cake*

ALSACE

Although Linzertorte is really an Austrian speciality, it is also eaten in this part of France, where raspberries grow in ripe profusion. The Germanic influence on the cooking, seen here in the use of the cinnamon-spiced pastry, is very strong.

Preparation time: 30 minutes (plus 1 hour resting)
Cooking time: 35 to 40 minutes
Oven temperature: 180°C, 350°F, Gas Mark 4
To serve: 6 to 8

100 g/4 oz butter
100 g/4 oz sugar
1 small egg
finely grated rind of ½ lemon
200 g/7 oz plain flour
1 teaspoon ground cinnamon
½ teaspoon ground cloves
pinch of salt
100 g/4 oz ground almonds
225 g/8 oz raspberries
1 tablespoon caster sugar

Cream the butter and sugar together and beat in the egg and the lemon rind. Sift the flour, cinnamon, cloves and salt into a bowl, then add gradually to the creamed mixture with the ground almonds. Gather the dough into a ball, cover and chill for 1 hour.

Roll out about two-thirds of the dough about 5 mm/¼ inch thick and use to line a 23 cm/9 inch flan tin,preferably a loose bottomed tin placed on a baking sheet. Spoon on the raspberries and sprinkle with the remaining sugar. Roll out the remaining dough and cut into strips 1 cm/½ inch wide. Make a lattice pattern over the tart. Seal the ends of the dough strips well into the edge of the tart.

Bake until the pastry is pale brown. Serve warm or cold.

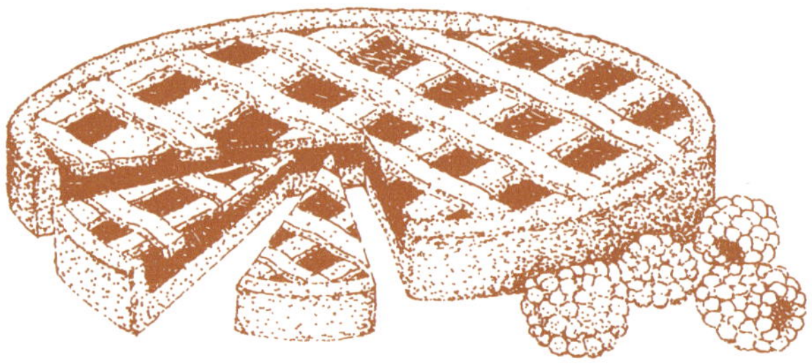

Kugelhopf *Yeast Cake*

ALSACE

Kugelhopf, Gugelhopf, Kougelhof, or Kugelhupf – whichever way you spell it, this light fruit cake or bread is one of the glories of Alsatian cooking. To look authentic, it should be baked in the slantingly fluted Kugelhopf ring mould, and should rise well above the mould during cooking.

Preparation time: 30 minutes (plus up to 2 hours rising)
Cooking time: 45 minutes
Oven temperature: 180°C, 350°F, Gas Mark 4
To serve: 6 to 8

50 g/2 oz raisins
1 tablespoon kirsch or warm water
15 g/½ oz fresh yeast
275 g/10 oz plain flour, sifted
50 g/2 oz caster sugar
5 tablespoons lukewarm milk
pinch of salt
2 eggs, beaten
125 g/4½ oz butter, melted and cooled
50 g/2 oz almonds, cut into slivers
1 tablespoon icing sugar

Soak the raisins in the kirsch or warm water.

Cream the yeast with 1 teaspoon of the flour and of the sugar. Add the warm milk. Cover and leave in a warm place until frothy.

Sift the remaining flour, salt and sugar into a bowl. Make a well in the centre and pour in the frothy yeast mixture. Add the eggs and the melted butter. Begin to work in the flour with a wooden spoon, then turn out and knead on a lightly floured surface until the dough becomes elastic and comes away from the surface.

Put back into the lightly floured bowl, sprinkle with a little flour, cover with a clean cloth and leave to rise in a warm place for at least 1 hour, or until it has doubled in bulk.

Knock back and form into a fat sausage shape. Sprinkle on half the drained raisins and the almonds. Fold over and add the remaining raisins and almonds. Fold over once more and fit into the well-buttered kugelhopf mould (the mixture should not come more than halfway up). Leave to rise again until the mixture has doubled once more and risen to the top of the mould.

Bake for about 45 minutes. The top should have risen well above the top of the mould and should be light and springy to the touch. If the top appears to be browning too quickly, cover with a piece of buttered foil.

Allow the cake to cool for a few minutes, then turn out onto a wire cake rack and dust liberally with icing sugar.

Baba Au Rhum *Rum Baba*

LORRAINE

Legend has it that Stanilaus Leczinski, deposed King of Poland – later to become the father-in-law of Louis XV, and to whom Nancy owes its elegant Place Stanislas – introduced the baba to France. The Arabian Nights were the source of his inspiration.

Preparation time: 2 hours
Cooking time: 20 minutes
Oven temperature: 220°C, 425°F, Gas Mark 7
To serve: 6 to 8

15 g/$\frac{1}{2}$ oz fresh yeast
25 g/1 oz caster sugar
150 ml/$\frac{1}{4}$ pint warm milk
225 g/8 oz flour
pinch of salt
4 eggs
100 g/4 oz butter, melted and cooled

Syrup
175 g/6 oz sugar
450 ml/$\frac{3}{4}$ pint water
2 strips of lemon rind
4 tablespoons rum
To decorate:
150 ml/$\frac{1}{4}$ pint crème chantilly (see page 121) or lightly whipped cream
glacé cherries

Cream the yeast with half the sugar and stir in the milk. Leave for 5 minutes in a warm place until frothy.

Sift the flour and salt into a warmed bowl and make a well in the centre. Pour the yeast mixture into the centre of the flour, and using a wooden spoon gradually work the flour into the liquid. Knead or beat with a wooden spoon for 5 minutes, until the dough becomes elastic and leaves the sides of the bowl clean. Cover with a damp cloth. Leave to rise in a warm place until the dough to twice its original volume.

Butter some baba pans or small cylindrical moulds.

Beat the eggs with the remaining sugar and pour in the butter. Beat this mixture slowly into the dough and continue to beat until the dough becomes smooth and glossy. Half fill each mould and leave to rise again in a warm place or until the dough has risen to the tops of the moulds. Place in the oven and bake until the tops of the babas are lightly browned and quite firm to the touch, and they have shrunk slightly from the sides of their pans. Leave to cool a little, then turn out of the pans and leave to cool on a wire rack.

Meanwhile dissolve the sugar in the water in a saucepan, add the lemon rind and bring to the boil. Boil for 5 minutes. Leave to cool, then remove the strips of lemon rind from the syrup and add 3 tablespoons of the rum.

When the babas are still just warm, place them on a large dish and gently spoon the syrup over each one. The babas should be allowed to absorb as much syrup as they can without losing their shape. Leave to cool.

Just before serving sprinkle a little of the remaining rum over each one. Top each baba with a swirl of crème chantilly or whipped cream and crown with a cherry.

Tarte Alsacienne Au Rhubarbe *Alsatian Rhubarb Tart*

ALSACE

The creamy filling counteracts the sharpness of the rhubarb in this lovely mellow tart, which may be served as a dessert or at teatime, but will need to be eaten with pastry forks.

Preparation time: 30 minutes (plus pastry)
Cooking time: 50 minutes
Oven temperature: 190°C, 375°F, Gas Mark 5
To serve: 6

0.75 kg/1$\frac{1}{2}$ lb rhubarb, trimmed and cut into 2.5 cm/1 inch lengths
175 g/6 oz sugar
225 g/8 oz pâte brisée sucrée (see page 114)
3 eggs, separated
4 tablespoons crème fraîche (see page 118) or double cream
finely grated rind of $\frac{1}{2}$ lemon

Sprinkle the prepared rhubarb with half the sugar and leave for about 30 minutes to draw out the juice.

Meanwhile roll out the pastry and use to line a buttered 25 cm/10 inch flan tin. Prick it well all over and bake blind for 10 minutes.

Drain the rhubarb, reserving the juice, and arrange it in a single layer in the pastry case. Sprinkle with half the remaining sugar and return to the oven. Bake for 20 minutes, or until the rhubarb begins to soften.

Beat the egg yolks with the remaining sugar and beat in the rhubarb juice and the cream. Add the lemon rind. Beat the egg whites until stiff but not dry. Fold into the egg yolk mixture and pour this over the rhubarb.

Return the tart to the oven and bake for a further 20 minutes, or until the filling has set. Serve warm, or cold.

Les Macarons Macaroons

BEARN

Macaroons should be light, crisp on the outside and soft and moist inside. They should not be too sweet, and in the south of France a few bitter almonds or cracked peach or apricot kernels are often added to the almonds to give a slightly bitter tang. A similar effect can be achieved by using some unblanched almonds.

Preparation time: 10 minutes
Cooking time: 15 to 20 minutes
Oven temperature: 190°C, 375°F, Gas Mark 5
To serve: 8 or more

225 g/8 oz almonds (see above), finely ground
400 g/15 oz caster sugar
½ teaspoon ground rice or cornflour
4 egg whites
rice paper
split blanched almonds or halved glacé cherries to decorate (optional)

Mix together the almonds, sugar and ground rice or cornflour in a bowl. Add the egg whites and combine thoroughly with a wooden spoon. Leave for a few minutes, then beat again briefly. Spread sheets of rice paper on baking sheets, rough side down. Using a teaspoon, make little mounds of the almond mixture on the sheets, leaving plenty of space between each one, to allow room for the macaroons to spread.

Press a split almond or half a glacé cherry in the centre of each one, if you like. Bake in the oven for 15 to 20 minutes. Do not overcook, as the macaroons should be light and dry on the outside, but slightly tacky in the centre.

Remove from the oven, break off each macaroon from the sheets of paper and leave to cool on a wire rack. Crumble off any surplus rice paper around the edges before serving.

Dacquoise *Hazelnut Meringue Layer Cake*

BEARN

Like most self-respecting French towns, the spa town of Dax, near the Spanish border, has its own speciality. This light and delectable cake is quite simple to make, but can be decorated to look very impressive.

Preparation time: 1 hour
Cooking time: 1 hour for the meringue and 20 minutes for the butter cream
Oven temperature: 140°C, 275°F, Gas Mark 1
To serve: 6 to 8

Dacquoise, parfait Marie Brizard, les macarons and St Emilion au chocolat (page 141)

Meringue Base
6 egg whites
pinch of salt
¼ teaspoon cream of tartar
175 g/6 oz caster sugar
1 tablespoon cornflour
75 g/3 oz ground almonds
75 g/3 oz ground hazelnuts

Butter Cream
4 egg yolks
100 g/4 oz caster sugar
300 ml/½ pint milk
175 g/6 oz unsalted butter
3 tablespoon kirsch, rum or very strong black coffee
50 g/2 oz plain or bitter chocolate, melted and cooled
100 g/4 oz powdered praline (see Croquante, page 127)

To decorate
50 g/2 oz toasted flaked almonds

Beat the egg whites with the salt until they begin to get foamy, then beat in the cream of tartar. Continue beating until the whites begin to stand in peaks, then start adding the sugar a spoonful at a time and continue until all the sugar has been absorbed and the meringue is smooth and bulky. Sift the cornflour and the ground nuts together and gradually fold into the meringue using a spatula or metal spoon, and being careful not to let the meringue mixture loose air.

Butter and lightly flour two baking sheets, or line them with rice paper, and spoon on the meringue mixture, spreading and smoothing it to make two equal 20–25 cm/10–12 inch diameter rounds. Place in the centre of the oven and bake for 1 hour, changing the meringue rounds over half way through cooking until just firm to the touch and very slightly browned.

Leave to cool a little on a wire rack, then remove from the baking sheets or rice papers.

Make the butter cream by beating the egg yolks together with the sugar until pale. Bring the milk just to the boil, then pour onto the egg mixture in a thin stream, still beating. Pour into a clean pan and stir over a very gentle heat until the custard begins to thicken. Do not allow to boil. Pour back into the mixing bowl and allow to cool a little.

Cut the butter into small pieces and add them to the custard one by one, beating all the time, until all the butter has been absorbed. Beat in the kirsch, rum or coffee.

Pour half the mixture into another bowl, add the melted chocolate and beat until smooth. Add the powdered praline to the other half. Leave to cool.

When the two butter creams are quite cooled, sandwich the two meringue rounds together with the praline cream and decorate the top with the chocolate cream and flaked almonds.

Gâteau De Savoie *Sponge Cake*

SAVOIE

This is an excellent, simple sponge cake which can be eaten alone, or served to accompany fruit or ices. It may also be sandwiched together with some crème chantilly (see page 121) and soft fruit.

Preparation time: 20 minutes
Cooking time: 40 to 45 minutes
Oven temperature: 190°C, 375°F, Gas Mark 5
To serve: 6 to 8

6 large eggs, separated
225 g/8 oz caster sugar
1 tablespoon orange flower water or water
75 g/3 oz plain flour
75 g/3 oz cornflour or potato starch
pinch of salt

Beat the egg yolks with the sugar and orange flower water or water until light, pale and bulky. Sift the flour together with the cornflour or potato starch and salt and carefully fold into the egg yolk mixture.

Whisk the whites until they stand in peaks, then fold into the cake mixture. Divide between two greased and floured sandwich tins and bake until the cakes are just firm to the touch and have slightly shrunk away from the sides of the tin. Turn out and leave to cool before serving or sandwiching together with cream.

Gâteaux A Noix *Walnut and Chocolate Slices*

AUVERGNE

The Auvergne is a walnut-growing area, and every *pâtisserie* has its own walnut speciality, such as these rich but light cream and chocolate-covered slices.

Preparation time: 40 minutes (plus pastry and chilling)
Cooking time: 40 to 45 minutes
Oven temperature: 190°C, 375°F, Gas Mark 5
To serve: 6 to 8

½ quantity pâte brisée sucrée (see page 114)
3 eggs
2 tablespoons hot strong black coffee (made with instant coffee)
175 g/6 oz soft brown sugar
50 g/2 oz unsalted butter, melted and cooled
75 g/3 oz plain flour, sifted
100 g/4 oz shelled walnuts, fairly finely chopped

Topping
65 g/2½ oz unsalted butter
175 g/6 oz icing sugar
2 tablespoons strong black coffee
125 g/5 oz plain eating chocolate
1 tablespoon cream

Roll out the dough and use to line a 20 × 30 cm/8 × 12 inch cake tin. Bake blind for 15 minutes near the top of the oven.

Meanwhile beat the eggs with the hot coffee and sugar until thick and fluffy. Gently fold in the butter and flour and then the walnuts. Pour this mixture into the pastry case and spread evenly. Return to the oven and bake for 25 to 30 minutes or until set. Leave to cool.

To make the topping, beat 50 g/2 oz of the butter with the icing sugar and coffee until smooth. Spread thinly over the cooled cake and chill to help the buttercream to set.

Break the chocolate into a heatproof bowl. Add the cream and set over a pan of simmering water. Stir until melted and smooth, then add the remaining butter cut into small pieces. Leave to cool, then spread evenly over the buttercream on the cake and leave to set. Cut the cake into squares before serving.

Poirat De Berry *Peppered Pear Tart*

BERRY

A piquant speciality of Berry, this is known locally as *piquenchagne*. The pepper just lifts the flavour in an unexpectedly pleasant way.

Preparation time: 30 minutes (plus 1 hour marinating)
Cooking time: 30 to 35 minutes
Oven temperature: 190°C, 375°F, Gas Mark 5
To serve: 4 to 6

0.5 kg/1 lb pears, peeled and cut into eighths
1 tablespoon brandy or eau-de-vie de marc
2 tablespoons sugar
just under ½ quantity pâte brisée sucrée (see page 114)
finely ground black pepper
150 ml/¼ pint crème fraîche (see page 118) or double cream

Sprinkle the pears with the brandy and 1 tablespoon of the sugar and leave for about 1 hour.

Roll out the dough and use to line a 20 cm/8 inch flan tin. Prick the base and bake blind for 10 minutes.

Drain the pears, reserving the brandy, and lay them evenly in the pastry case. Sprinkle with the remaining sugar, dust lightly with pepper and bake until the pastry is cooked and the pears are tender.

Mix the brandy in which the pears have soaked with the cream. When the pears are cooked, pour the brandy mixture over the tart and return to the oven for another 5 minutes cooking to set.

Serve warm or cold.

St Emilion Au Chocolat *Chocolate Macaroon Dessert*

GUYENNE

The town of St. Emilion, near Bordeaux, is not only a great centre for wine-growing, but has also lent its name to this rich chocolate dessert made with macaroons, which are one of the town's specialities.

Preparation time: 30 minutes plus chilling overnight
To serve: 8 to 10

100 g/4 oz unsalted butter
100 g/4 oz caster sugar
150 ml/¼ pint milk
1 egg yolk
200 g/7 oz bitter or plain eating chocolate
1 batch macaroons (see page 138)
3 tablespoons brandy or Armagnac
Decoration (optional):
150 ml/¼ pint whipped cream
chocolate shavings

Decoration
150 ml/¼ pint whipped cream
chocolate shavings

Cream the butter and sugar together until very light and fluffy. Bring the milk almost to the boil, then mix a little of it into the egg yolk, to form a smooth cream. Break up the chocolate and add to the milk remaining in the saucepan. Return to a low heat and stir until the chocolate has completely melted and the mixture is absolutely smooth. Add the egg and stir until smooth. Slowly beat this chocolate cream into the butter and sugar mixture, and beat until the mixture is very light and smooth.

Arrange a layer of macaroons in the bottom of a glass or soufflé dish. Sprinkle with a little brandy or Armagnac. Smooth on a layer of the chocolate cream. Repeat until everything has been used up, ending with macaroons. Leave in the refrigerator overnight to mature. Decorate, if you like, with a layer of whipped cream, sprinkled with chocolate shavings, before serving.

Pavé Aux Marrons *Chocolate Chestnut Cake*

GUYENNE

This is a very rich cake, which can be eaten as a dessert or as a confection. The mixture can also be shaped into a yule log, decorated with a fork to give the appearance of bark, sprinkled with a little icing sugar to look like snow, and decorated with hazelnuts for knots in the bark.

Preparation time: 15 minutes (plus peeling chestnuts)
Cooking time: 20 minutes
To serve: 6

0.75 kg/1½ lb chestnuts, peeled
100 g/4 oz caster sugar
100 g/4 oz plain or bitter eating chocolate
100 g/4 oz unsalted butter

Icing
100 g/4 oz plain or bitter eating chocolate
1 tablespoon water
15 g/½ oz butter

Put the chestnuts into a large heavy saucepan, cover with cold water and bring to the boil. Simmer for about 20 minutes, or until they are tender. Drain and purée in a blender or mouli-légumes. Fold the sugar into the purée and leave to cool.

Melt the chocolate in a heatproof basin set over a pan of simmering water. Remove from the pan and stir until smooth, then add the butter, cut into small pieces, and stir until well combined. Work this into the chestnut mixture until you have a soft, smooth mixture.

Turn into a greased and lined cake tin and chill overnight. Ice with the chocolate melted with the water and butter, and cut into squares when set.

Or chill the mixture, then form into a yule log and leave overnight to set. Streak with the melted chocolate icing and decorate as suggested above.

Serve with brandy-flavoured crème chantilly (see page 121) if liked.

Clafoutis Aux Cerises *Baked Cherry Pudding*

LIMOUSIN

Clafoutis, a baked batter pudding with fruit, are eaten throughout France. This recipe comes from the Limousin, where some of the best cherries grow. Ripe but firm black cherries should be used.

Preparation time: 25 minutes (plus 1 hour marinating)
Cooking time: 40 to 45 minutes
Oven temperature: 220°C, 425°F, Gas Mark 7
To serve: 6

0.5 kg/1 lb black cherries, stoned
2 tablespoons kirsch or brandy
3 eggs
50 g/2 oz sugar
75 g/3 oz flour, sifted
pinch of salt
300 ml/½ pint milk
50 g/2 oz butter
icing sugar

Leave the cherries to soak in the kirsch or brandy for at least 1 hour.

Beat the eggs together with the sugar, then mix in the flour and salt, followed by the milk and half the butter, melted.

Butter a shallow ovenproof dish or cake tin very generously and pour in a thin layer of the batter. Bake for 5 minutes or until just set.

Drain the cherries and distribute them evenly over the batter. Pour the cherry liquid into the remaining batter, beat again and pour over the cherries. Dot with the remaining butter.

Return to the oven and bake until the top is set and lightly browned. Sprinkle generously with icing sugar and serve warm.

Index

Italic numerals refer to colour photographs